D0648376

KISS

YOURSELF

HELLO!

KISS YOURSELF *HELLO!*

From A Life Of Business
To The Business Of Life

A PERSONAL JOURNEY

Phil Parker

GOLDENeight Publishers
Atlanta * Toronto

Copyright © 1999 by Phil Parker
Cover Design: Lightbourne Images
Authors photographs: John Armstrong Photography
Edited: Sue Johnson

Printed by the University of Toronto Press

ISBN #1-890412-69-4

Library of Congress Cataloging: #98-075593

GOLDENeight Publishers
2778 Cumberland Blvd
Suite: 206
Smyrna, GA 30080 USA

DEDICATION

I dedicate this book to my wife and soulmate…
Bonnie Ross-Parker

Of all the possibilities, I've been blessed with the best.

You give me light in moments of darkness.
You give me encouragement in times of doubt.
Your unwaivering support gives me confidence.
Your unconditional caring, and concern for others frees
my spirit.
Your insights open my mind.
Your love nourishes my soul.

I am a fortunate man.

I LOVE YOU

TO MY CHILDREN

Jason Scott Parker and Lisa Faye Parker

This book is for you.

Dad loves you.

SPECIAL ACKNOWLEDGEMENTS

To my brother Bruce J. Parker whose love I cherish, whose voice lights up my day and whose humor always makes my soul laugh. I love you, Bro.

To my in-laws Lillian and Robert Renert for their unconditional love and support.

To Elizabeth Ross Lieberman and Glenn David Ross who have brought so much enthusiasm, encouragement, support and love into my life.

To my family and friends who have followed my life with bewilderment.

In loving memory of my parents
Rose and Jerry Parker

ACKNOWLEDGEMENTS

Writing a book is like producing a play. The central character receives most of the recognition; however the play's success is largely determined by the entire supporting cast.

While this book chronicles my personal journey, it represents the collaborative input of family, friends and colleagues. My thanks to the following people who continue to enrich my life:

Cindy and Alan Goldsberry for encouraging me to stretch my imagination.

Rosemary and Manny Hammelberg who challenged me to begin the task.

Lynn and Stephen Gower for trusting our new friendship through their openness and candor.

Colin Tipping for framing and crystalizing my ideas.

Willie Jolley for his inspiration.

Dr. Allan Somersall for both his enthusiasm and editorial insights.

My dear Canadian friend and literary agent extraordinaire, Carolina Loren, who laughs at my jokes and keeps me on schedule.

Rene Godefroy, a special person and gifted speaker, who gave freely of his time, endless support, and continuous encouragement.

My daughter-in-law Andrea Kleinman-Parker and my son-in-law Ron Lieberman for showing me how much family cares.

My friends in The Peoples Network for love and motivation.

To my fellow Toastmasters (Speaker's Roundtable) for their support.

To my professional colleagues of the National Speakers Association and The Georgia Speakers Association for friendship and advice.

To Michael, J.R., and the staff at my local bookstore for providing bagels, coffee and conversation.

THE MISSION OF THIS BOOK IS TO ENRICH, ENLIGHTEN, AND ENCOURAGE OTHERS TO DISCOVER THEIR LIFE'S PURPOSE IN ORDER TO ACHIEVE PERSONAL GROWTH AND SIGNIFICANCE.

TABLE OF CONTENTS

TABLE OF CONTENTS

Chapters   **Page No.**

FOREWORD

Having produced this book, I guess it makes me an author. To be honest with you though, I don't really think of myself as such. I know myself better as a motivational speaker. That's how I make my living.

The fact is, I am very comfortable standing in front of a group of people talking about life. I'm naturally funny and entertaining, and I love the work. Companies seem to be convinced that what I have to say is not only entertaining but also good for their bottom line. Writing, on the other hand, seems like hard work to me and not nearly as enjoyable. Nevertheless, I wrote this book. Why?

Every project begins with a creative urge. Such inspiration usually arises out of some incident, emotion, insight or vision. For me, it was purely emotional – at least in the beginning. Yes, I knew being a published author would enhance my speaking career, but that in itself would never have been motivation enough for me to do what didn't come naturally.

I am clear now that my creative urge came from a mixture of repressed anger, frustration and guilt. These emotions had accumulated over a long period of time, mostly the result of what I perceived as my failures in life, in business, in marriage, and in general. But I was not conscious of these emotions and I would never admit to having them. I certainly never thought of myself as an *angry* person – quite the opposite, in fact.

It was only later during the writing process that I was to discover that I was upset with Corporate America and why. Initially, I saw the American business culture as a manipulative, exploitive system that lured you in, drained you dry and deserted you in the end with little or no personal reward. In reality, I was responsible for my own frustration and lack of fulfillment and unjustly blamed Corporate America.

For a long time, I was unable to see my own part in my dissatisfaction and failed to take responsibility for the choices I had made during my thirty-five years in the corporate world. I was a victim, pure and simple, and I was going to let the whole world know about it! Ironically, this book is not only an account of how I came to terms with all that negative emotion but it is a testimony to how the writing of it became an entirely transformational process for me. Let me explain.

At the time I decided to write this book, I was fifty-six years of age, jobless, unemployable, pretty much broke, and more depressed than I knew. I was self-righteous enough to believe that the reason I was writing a book was to save all the young people about to enter Corporate America from becoming victims of **the system.** The title was going to be *Where's Your Gold Watch?* So sure of the title, I printed business cards and other promotional material.

But as I began writing, slowly and surely my frame of mind began to shift -- and with it the book. Instead of being an attack on Corporate America, it evolved into a story of self-discovery. It became my personal vehicle for intense growth and transformation. In reality, it never was going to be a book to rescue other people from their fate. It was a book that would ultimately rescue **me** – from myself.

So, yes, even though I was the last to realize it, the book was really for me all along. Yet, I am inviting you along for the journey. I believe my search for meaning in my life is much like everyone else's, and you may well find something of yourself in it.

My story may move you. It may precipitate change. If it allows you to become more of who you really are, instead of who others say you should be, it will have served a divine purpose. I believe that much of the unhappiness and stress in the world is caused by too many people living lives out of alignment with their true nature. Instead, they live according to a whole string of oughts, shoulds, and other people's rules, doing work they were not really cut out to do. That's wrong and it is sad. It is now time to break free and

finally become ourselves!

Phil Parker, 1999

PART ONE

CONFESSIONS

I have come a long way.
You have probably done that too.
It is my turn to speak.
It is your time to think.

1

FACE TO FACE

**"You are today where your thoughts
have brought you;
You will be tomorrow where your
thoughts take you."**

James Allen

One evening shortly before my 57th birthday and following a memorable Italian dinner, I was taking a slow stroll through my Atlanta neighborhood. Enjoying the sights and sounds of spring, I lit my favorite briarwood pipe. I could smell the sweet and aromatic cherry vanilla tobacco in the still summer air. Birds were singing. The dogwoods were in full bloom and the azaleas were just reaching their stunning red and white color. I was feeling great! Life was good! Suddenly, without warning, a nagging and recurring thought engulfed my mind.

Who Am I?

Why it came back into my head at that precise moment is beyond me. I had been alone before. Walking after dinner had been a regular habit. This neighborhood was familiar and recent events in my life had not been unusual. My mood was normal and no one had commented on my demeanor of late. So why did this penetrating question arise?

I could find no obvious precipitating factor. Yet it was not one of those fleeting, *why me* kinds of thoughts that sometimes wander through our minds in moments of quiet solitude and periods of self-reflection. Actually, I began wrestling with that question many years earlier but either could not nor chose not to confront it. Suddenly, it had confronted me.

It was like being hit by a comet. Never before in my life had I been overcome with any idea in this way. It was a dark shadow, projected from deep in the core of my being, enveloping my body. It erupted in my mind like a giant volcano and it left a deep crater to be filled. My spirit seemed like a devastated wasteland. Suddenly, it seemed to me that all of the things that identified who I was and defined my purpose in society were without foundation. I was shaken up. I felt vulnerable and alienated, even from myself.

Now, let me assure you, I am not any kind of air-head! Others have always considered me a regular kind of guy with my feet firmly on the ground — rational, logical and a down to earth family man. Admittedly, I knew nothing of the paranormal; nor felt strongly religious or spiritual. This was definitely new territory for me.

My head was spinning, my mind was cluttered and I was feeling very unsteady. I looked around and I saw I was still alone. "Thank God," I thought. I almost felt naked, as though I had been stripped of my camouflage. After all, if I was uncertain of who I was after being my constant companion for almost 57 years, how could I be certain of anything?

"Who am I?" The very substance of the idea scared me. Oddly enough, I felt a sense of exhilaration. It was as if a bright light had been turned on – or maybe off – I was not sure which.

I felt myself trembling as I sat down on an old, beat up, wooden park bench. It felt good to have something solid beneath me!

"What does this mean? How can I not know who I am?" I asked myself. "Why is this idea hitting me so hard and with such profundity?"

The truth was, of course, I had no idea what it meant. I did not know where it was going to lead me. However, what I did know, with an absolute certainty I had never experienced before, was that nothing was ever going to be the same again. Something very important had happened and I knew it was going to have an impact on the rest of my life. It was the beginning of a complete makeover, not in the cosmetic sense but, rather, from within.

2

Worldly Welcome

"We are all born crying, live complaining, and die disappointed."

Thomas Fuller

The original Phil Parker, at the most authentic he was ever going to be – at least for the next 59 years – made his debut into the world as Philip Gary Parker on May 10, 1939. The roller coaster ride had begun.

Franklin D. Roosevelt was President. It was the year that Britain and France declared war on Germany, Byron Nelson won the U.S. Open golf title, and illness forced Lou Gehrig to retire from baseball. Nylon offered the promise of sheer elegant stockings for all women. The top songs of the day were "Over The Rainbow" and "Beer Barrel Polka". Theaters were showing "Gone With The Wind" and "The Wizard of Oz." Bobby Hull, the hockey Hall of Famer, was born.

I was born before television, before the availability of penicillin, Xerox machines, credit cards and even *the pill*. While I have always loved music, I was born before anyone had ever heard of FM, tape decks, compact disks, or even hi-fidelity. When I entered this world, "made in Japan" meant junk. There were no electric typewriters, word processors, or computers let alone cellular phones, pagers, the Internet or the World Wide Web. WWW stood for Wild Wild West as Roy Rogers was becoming King of the Cowboys with Gene Autry crooning his signature song, "I'm Back In The Saddle Again."

Cigarette smoking (not cigar smoking), was fashionable and not considered bad for your health. Grass was something you mowed, Coke was a soft drink, and pot was a cooking utensil. People got married first and then lived together. Closets were for putting clothes in and not for "coming out" of.

It's incredible how quickly the world has changed.

I have little recollection of my first thoughts upon entering the world. Therefore, I have no idea whether my first thoughts were more in the realm of *Wow, this process was easy and life is OK,* or, *This experience pales compared to the warmth of the womb during the last nine months.*

Recently I have come to learn, through the writings of Stanislav Grof and other researchers in the so-called rebirthing movement, that these very first thoughts can be crucial to the way we view life and can influence our basic approach to living from that day foreword.

Reflecting on the life I created in my first fifty-seven years, I probably entered the world thinking, *Gee, getting here was one hell of a struggle and when I arrived the only reward I got was a slap on my backside and a plastic wrist bracelet. Then I'm wrapped in a blanket, assigned a number, dumped in a crib, and left to feel lonely and abandoned. This is not a very friendly world!*

While sharing a sense of my turbulent entrance into this world and the great struggle (World War II) that existed at the time, perhaps it is also appropriate to share the realization and continuing saga of my own life struggle. I never understood or admitted to myself that I, too, would be engaged in a great, self-contained conflict to discover my own purpose, passion, and significance while the world was fighting for its own survival and its own future.

Not remembering much of my childhood, I began to reflect on my early adult life for clues as to who I was and what I had become.

Having been told for years by friends and family alike that I seem to enjoy a *living on the edge* lifestyle always caused me to chuckle. Even to this day I always sleep on the edge of the bed, sit on the edge of the chair, tip toe across the floor and try to stay on the cutting edge of fashion. To those who knew me, it appeared to be an exciting lifestyle. For me, it was the only way I knew how to function. Looking back from where I am now, living on the edge was my way of avoiding both life's challenges and opportunities.

In the eyes of some, I had limited success. After all, I had been a corporate executive. I had won some and lost some. Yet, in my own eyes, I had fought off the waves of the business world but swallowed much of its rejection and self-effacement in the process. I had been up and I had been down, but I was always in the game.

I had made my life a struggle. I was always paddling like hell to get somewhere, but I did not know where I was going and would not have had a clue if I had gotten there. Many years later, seeing myself as a volunteer victim of the corporate culture, I labeled myself a failure financially and in the world of business.

It became obvious to me that I had to make some

significant changes in my life. If I failed to do so, in a few more years I would be living on a meager social security allowance, with the benefits of Medicare and senior citizen discounts for movies and air travel. That script might never have changed had it not been for two things – my second marriage and my self-awakening that evening during my neighborhood stroll.

My *living on the edge* lifestyle had both guided and misguided me through fifty-seven years. I chose to relinquish its reins to pursue a creative and more significant lifestyle that would propel me with purpose into the twenty-first century.

For me, growing up in Scranton, Pennsylvania during the fifties was great fun. With its closed businesses, boarded up houses, and sinking streets, Scranton today is a city struggling for its economic life. Like many small cities of the fifties, Scranton has not kept up with change very well and the city is a skeleton of what it used to be. But, beneath this modern day sleepy hollow lies the spirit and friendliness of an important asset: its residents. The citizens of Scranton are proud to be who they are and there is a strong kinship between us. To this day, I remain close to many of my friends from those years. While my children have a difficult time believing I was born and raised in Scranton, I am proud to say I am a Scrantonian.

Without middle school in those days, I attended John James Audubon elementary school in Scranton through the eighth grade. My high school years were occupied with athletic endeavors, a serious romance, and Dick Clark's *American Bandstand*. Rock and Roll was here to stay. My participation in sports and my romance with my high school sweetheart filled all of my time and energy. I still love sports, but my teenage romance ended while I was in the Navy. I will share this story with you later.

Throughout my high school years I struggled with the curriculum that most high schools offered. You know what they are. I was an average student but discovered that studying on a regular basis was not for me. As I recall, there wasn't any subject that turned me on or any teacher I could call a mentor. I simply staggered my way through four years.

3

IN SEARCH OF SIGNIFICANCE

**"We must take charge of our lives.
Each one of us must act
to restore the balance".**

Duane Elgin

It had been almost two months since my walk in the neighborhood. My 57th birthday had come and gone. My two children, Jason and Lisa, dutifully called to wish me a happy birthday as did Elizabeth and Glenn, my wife's children from her previous marriage. Bonnie and I went out for a cozy, inexpensive dinner at our favorite Chinese restaurant. True to habit, I devoured my usual Kung Pao chicken and Bonnie, a vegetarian, enjoyed her predictable choice of steamed mixed vegetables.

At dinner Bonnie mentioned that I appeared pensive and not quite my normal self. She was closer to the truth than she realized. Other than her observation, nobody seemed to notice anything different about me. I surely felt different, though. The nagging feeling of not understanding myself continued. I was not equipped to share my thoughts with Bonnie. The fleeting thought that I was becoming psychotic even crossed my mind, but frankly, I didn't feel there was anything amiss with me. Quite the contrary, I was feeling better and more positive than ever before. It was a light feeling of slowly being relieved of a heavy burden, like the feeling of relief after spending the entire weekend cleaning out the closets and garage.

I wondered if I should share my thoughts with my wife. At times during our two years of marriage, we had discussed my overall lack of financial success, low self-regard and lack of confidence. Emotionally, this was of a different magnitude and I knew I was not well-equipped for the pain of a soul-searching discussion. I had never attended any of those fashionable *bare-your-soul* and *let-it-all-hang-out* seminars in the fifties or sixties; so I had neither the right vocabulary nor thought process. I retreated, deciding to remain silent.

It was much later when I discovered that my thoughts and accompanying feelings were not unusual. It was simply symptomatic of realizing **my** age. Yes, I was experiencing male menopause. True, it was a long time coming. Obviously, I resisted or did not acknowledge life's changes earlier. My denial mechanism had been working overtime.

Middle age had tip toed up on me and had just about passed when it jolted me. What a surprise! There is an expression, *when the pupil is ready the teacher will appear*. I guess I was ready! Menopause was like an emotional volcano. This time I could not control the eruption as I had done in the past.

Later, I began to understand that all of us go through various stages of development in our lives, not only in childhood and adolescence, but in adulthood as well. When we resist change in our lives, we actually obstruct the normal process of life. Sooner or later, life has a way of bursting through our obstructions and denials with the spiritual equivalent of a sledgehammer. The best I can figure, that is what happened to me.

What is popularly known as a mid-life crisis is, in fact, life's way of forcing us to accept the changes that we have been resisting. If I had not been ignoring life and trying to control it, I probably would not have had the crisis. It was simply a case of ignorant resistance. For the first fifty years of my life, I just did not get the message. It is probably more accurate to say the message kept flashing across the neon sign in my mind, but I did not have the switch on.

Carl Jung, the famous Swiss psychiatrist, said that man spends the first forty years of his life integrating his ego (sense of self) by gaining mastery over his environment, creating material wealth and impacting social and political institutions. He then spends the second half of his life trying to break down his ego in order to gain mastery of himself. While the first half of life is outer-directed, the last half of life is inner-directed. The midlife crisis is symptomatic of the transition stage. The feelings of not knowing who you are or what your purpose is in life are, according to Jung, perfectly normal.

Of course, Dr. Jung and I were not intimately acquainted; so I struggled with the trauma on my own. I thought I was the only person in the world who felt this confusion. In an attempt to get a handle on my life, I found myself going back over my past trying to recall significant events that might provide some clues as to who I was and what I had become. It became important for me to discover what really mattered in my life's journey.

4

FAMILY MATTERS

**"Let neither work nor play,
no matter how satisfying or glorious,
ever separate me, for long, from the love
that unites my precious family."**

Og Mandino

Like many people my age, my memory is not always functioning on full power. Wanting to recall the most essential and formulative aspects of my early life in order to make sense of the present turned out to be a problem. I found I could barely remember anything about my childhood or preadolescence. My earliest recollections are around age fifteen. I vividly remember my full time participation in sports, my first true love affair, time spent with my brother and, of course, my parents. This is where I began my inquiry.

My mother was a caring and loving woman who aged graciously. All of five feet tall, she had silver hair, emerald-green eyes and an infectious smile. A typical wife of the forties and fifties, she stayed at home, raised her family, and made sure she always cooked a hot meal for dinner. She was gregarious, accepting of everybody and enjoyed her weekly mah jong game. Frequently, she went out for lunch with her friends.

One of ten children, she never found her own identity and lived to the expectations of others. Always subservient to her husband, she did not know how to balance a checkbook. She was a typical mother of '*the day*.'

As she aged, arthritis began to hamper her movements and I can vividly remember how crooked her fingers became. She never complained. Mother had been a smoker since her teens and died at home of breast cancer at the age of sixty-six.

After the funeral, I remember going back to my parents' apartment. The apartment, while small, had a beautiful screened porch. My father was sitting on the porch, and I went out to console him. He was emotionally uncomfortable and attempted to mask his feelings. It was the only time I ever saw him cry.

Having said I have a fuzzy recollection of my childhood, I do remember being acutely aware of my father as a "big shot" politician in a small town. Although he was an attorney, his involvement in local politics overshadowed his legal career. He usually took the cause of the underdog, had zero tolerance for excuses and was extremely direct and to the point.

It was very important for him to be respected by everyone and to be constantly reminded of his importance. His name was often in local newspapers and he appeared periodically on local television. His need for ego gratification and to feel appreciated and respected by his peers was obvious. As I reflect on life with my father, I wonder, in spite of all the outward recognition he got during his life, if my dad had any real sense of self beyond the clippings and the publicity he received.

Not being motivated by material wealth, but rather by the recognition and the respect of others, my father frequently gave away his legal expertise. Clients would call him at home during the evening hours and ask for advice, and he would spend hours on the telephone counseling the caller on legal matters. When I would ask him if he sent them a bill, he would reply, *"They are just friends who need some legal help."* While I was under the impression that all lawyers charged for their legal advice, my father was often the exception.

He was unique in other ways too. One day while playing golf, he felt a small lump on his left wrist. He paid little attention to it, but it increased in size after several months. He agreed to a biopsy. It was malignant.

Although it was not considered life threatening, Dad underwent several sessions of radiation therapy. The lump diminished and he assumed all was well. About six months later, the cancer reappeared and was diagnosed as life threatening. The medical team suggested that his arm be amputated slightly below the elbow. Fitted with a prosthesis, he would be fine. It was decision time! My dad's choice was to lose an arm and save his life, or do nothing. His was a life or death choice.

All his life my father was a fiercely independent man. For him the choice was clear. It was not the choice I would have made. He said, *"I came into this world a complete human being and that is exactly the way I choose to leave it."* He had made **his** choice. There was no discussion.

As the cancer spread to his shoulders and then to his lymph glands, he began to show visible signs of his illness. Chemotherapy slowed the process, but he continued to get weaker and weaker. In typical fashion, he refused to give up his independence and was never hospitalized. As his strength began to disappear, his bodily control deserted him. Around the clock in-home care became essential.

Bonnie and I visited him many times during the final year of his life. We watched him struggle to maintain his independence and self- dignity. His positive attitude never diminished. He kept his calendar full with meetings and appointments believing he would keep them all. He was an incredibly determined and strong-willed human being who reluctantly accepted help during the last few months of his life.

On May 29, 1991, the day of my brother's birthday, he passed away in his sleep. He was 79. The cause of death was listed as respiratory failure; cancer was the messenger.

I imagine my father could have lived another dozen years if he had made a different choice. Looking back, I realize that at the time of his death I was very angry with him for the choice he made. It was the right choice for him; it was the wrong choice for me. I wanted him to fight and not give in to the cancer because that is what I believe I would have done. At first, I could not forgive him. I did not want to lose my father. I still miss him and at the same time I had to let go and respect his life and his manner of dying. I understand that he did not owe it to me, my children, or to Scranton, Pennsylvania to hang on for a moment longer than he wanted. I have come to terms with his choice and learned to respect his decision to end his life the way he did.

His decision had a ripple effect. My brother and I lost our father, our children lost their grandfather and Scranton, Pennsylvania lost a compassionate and dedicated civic servant.

From an early age, I learned from my dad's example that outward success and visible recognition were true measures of one's worth. He used to say, "It doesn't matter what people say about you as long as they spell your name right." Did that mean that to be loved by him I had to achieve outward success and be recognized by others? I will never know the answer to that question.

Until recently, I had thought I did not crave recognition like my father. Recognition turned out to be one of my major denials. I now realize I, too, craved recognition and respect. Feeling the lack of both has been a problem in my life.

I often wonder whether our father's point of view affected my brother and me to the same degree. Even though I viewed my brother as successful, I felt quite the opposite. I have met many successful people who are happy, but I do not think I have met many who are happy only because they are successful. I believe that my father, in spite of his addiction to recognition, was happy and successful. He was generous and kind. His high need to receive was balanced by his willingness to give. He achieved significance during his lifetime and appeared fulfilled. His legacy is the *Jerry Parker Municipal Golf Course* located just outside Scranton. It was his labor of love. Built under a cloud of much public criticism, the golf course has raised millions of dollars for the city.

My brother, in contrast to my dad, does not show the need for recognition as a priority in his life. While he remains low-key about his own accomplishments, it is obvious that he has made some good choices in his life. I thought recognition did not matter much to me. I now know differently. My personal and professional lack of achievement has been eating away at me for a long time. While I am not jealous of my brother, I envy his professional status. He, like our father, is an attorney and the CEO of a large association in Washington, D.C. While both of us have experienced our individual challenges, personally and professionally, his list of accomplishments is undeniable. I cannot help comparing myself to him.

I love my brother. I think of him with great pride. I know he feels the same about me. Because we are geographically separated, we do not spend as much time together as I would like. In addition to his responsibilities at work, he has his hands full with two teenage daughters. We talk on the phone regularly and he constantly sends me humorous e-mail messages.

Recently, while having dinner with my brother and sister-in-law, he shared his perspective of our childhood years. I was amazed! We had grown up in the same house but his views of those years are significantly different from mine. I have also learned that each of my children view life from their own perspective.

My son Jason is very hard working. He possesses good business acumen and professional accomplishments have come to him easily. He is very focused and loves his work. Our relationship is not as close as I would like. We speak often, but our conversations are usually limited to sports and the stock market. I am working at strengthening our communication and our relationship.

His professional success reminds me of my own shortcomings and reinforces my guilt and dissatisfaction that I have not yet found peace within myself.

In that sense, Jason is a great teacher for me. When I get comfortable with myself, I know that he and I will be more comfortable with each other and share on a much deeper level. I look forward to that time and if this book is instrumental in speeding up the process, it will have been worth writing.

There are many questions in my mind that fear keeps me from asking: Does my son love me? Does he respect me in spite of my failed marriage to his mother? How does he view his childhood? How did divorce affect his view of life? Were his growing up years free from struggle, causing him to believe that life is easy? What part did I play in his upbringing to make him feel that success was his for the taking? Jason was the beneficiary of private schools and an expensive college education. Not unlike other parents, I had difficulty justifying the expense. As it turned out, the decision to provide him with a top-notch education was one of my better choices.

While I love and respect my son, our relationship has not been what I would like it to be. Perhaps he feels closer to me than he lets on but he does not wear his emotions on his shirt sleeves. He rarely asks me for advice. The truth is I am uneasy when we are together. I needed to share my feelings with him.

In September 1998, before attending a meeting in Dallas, Texas, Jason and I spent several hours together. I had requested the time to discuss my feelings, thoughts and some concerns. I was not judgmental. I just wanted to clear the air. We talked about my divorce from his mother, the college debt I incurred on his behalf, his relationship with his sister, his seeming lack of compassion and empathy towards others and the emotion I felt in his not attending my father's funeral. I was open and honest. Although I did most of the talking, he listened as I spoke. It was a cleansing experience for me and, I hope, enlightening for him.

My daughter Lisa is also my teacher but, of course, in a different way. She is cut from the fabric of my cloth and seems to understand me better. Everyone knows her as a caring person, with a wonderful sense of humor and brutal honesty. We do not always see eye to eye on family issues but we are, at least, able to discuss them. She chooses to follow her own path and is a very private person.

Lisa has been very supportive of me. On the passing of my father she flew from Atlanta, where she was living at the time, to Scranton, Pennsylvania to attend his funeral. She stays in touch on a regular basis either by phone or e-mail. Our conversations are usually philosophical and leave me smiling.

With the exception of my wife, Lisa has continued to be my strongest supporter. When I shared with her my plan to make a total career change and become both a speaker and author, she embraced the idea with wholehearted enthusiasm. Her response came as no surprise since she often wanted to hear my stories, share my experiences (although she doesn't believe most of them), and tell her friends about her world-traveler dad.

Seriously though, I do not think a conversation between us over the last several months ever failed to include her inquiring about the progress of my book. Her belief in me has been a major source of encouragement even on those days when writing was not in the forefront of my mind. As a matter-of-fact, Lisa was responsible for getting me my first speaking engagement.

Therefore, in totally different ways, this book not only represents my own personal growth but it will be a living legacy to the support and lessons I have received from both my children, each in their own unique way.

PERSONAL REFLECTIONS

5

CORPORATE MATTERS

**"Corporations are social organizations,
the theater in which men and women
realize or fail to realize
purposeful and productive lives."**

Peter Rena

B efore reading further, there are a few facts that I need to share with you.

I am not a Ph.D., an M.D., or even a CPA. I don't have my MBA, and I do not drive a BMW. Hell, I don't even have a J.O.B. I never say *been there and done that* since I don't know much of where I have been and hardly remember much of what I have done. I do recall what has been done to me.

I've been hired, fired, acquired, merged, purged, downsized, capsized and even rightsized. Defined, un-defined, and redefined, I've been outsourced, outscored, and even outlawed. Privatized, penalized, organized, and disorganized; I've been informed, uninformed, and asked to reform. I've been focused, unfocused, but mostly out of focus. You could say I've been left out, left off, and left behind. Each time I approached the goal line of success, the goal line moved.

It gets laughs and there is no doubt it has helped me get beyond my insecurities. Humor has probably helped others in much the same way. But it simply conceals my anger and frustration at never having been able to *make-it* in the corporate arena.

I have been told I am a great storyteller and can make people laugh. I have learned to use humor, especially self-deprecating humor, as a crutch to ease my emotional pain and lack of self-confidence. It is a good strategy to help camouflage my insecurities and mask my anger and frustrations.

My lack of purpose began with college. There was nothing exceptional about my college years. Having been accepted to the College of William and Mary, I lasted one year. Studying was an activity in which I rarely participated. Returning to Scranton and living at home with my parents, I enrolled in the University of Scranton. Attending classes on a somewhat irregular basis, I somehow managed to achieve passing grades.

In the fall of 1961, at age 22, I graduated with a major in Business Administration and a minor in Philosophy. As I walked across the stage to be blessed (it was a Jesuit University) as a college graduate and receive my diploma, I was also handed another piece of paper. It was a commission in the U.S. Navy. Not only was I a college graduate but also an *Officer and A Gentleman* by Act of Congress. I am not sure which document impressed me more.

Looking incredible in my Navy dress whites, I caught the eye of many young women. Of course I did not have a *gut* in those days, no visible *love handles* and my butt was a little higher off the ground. I was in peak physical condition. As a naval officer, I was usually a happy camper.

My naval orders sent me to an aircraft carrier in Alameda, California. This floating city weighed 83,000 tons. I had never seen a ship that large; it was almost as long as three football fields. The Captain, with four blazing gold stripes across his sleeve and a bunch of yellow gold (known as 'scrambled eggs') on the peak of his cap, was really the equivalent of today's CEO. His authority, competency, and responsibility could not be questioned.

The Navy was my first employer. It was my opportunity to tackle responsibility. I carried out my assignments and enjoyed my life as a naval officer. I took advantage of all the benefits and loved the travel. I never viewed the Navy as a corporation. Looking back, however, I discovered many organizational similarities. It did not take me long to realize that, in fact, it is one of the largest corporations in the world: It took control of my life.

I no longer had to make any daily decisions. The Navy decided when I would get up, what I would wear, most of what I ate, what my daily routine would be and when and how often I would travel. At the time, being in the Navy also created what I viewed as a crisis in my personal life. Let me explain.

While aboard the aircraft carrier USS Coral Sea (CVA-43) somewhere in the Pacific, I was the recipient of a *dear john* letter from my high school and college sweetheart of ten years. She informed me she was going to marry a local Scranton police officer. I was crushed. How could this happen to me? More importantly, what could I do about it? I was in a love-sick panic. I knew that I could be granted emergency leave for a family death or family emergency and this was it! The woman I loved was moving on with her life and marrying someone else. It was an emergency to me!

Believing I could stop the marriage and rekindle her love for me, I immediately went to the ship's Captain and pleaded my case for emergency leave. Without any discussion and obviously very little thought, the Captain denied my request. I can picture the expression of disbelief on his face and can remember his words, "Ensign Parker, you're in the United States Navy. Request denied."

I thought to myself, *that's it?* No explanation? No compassion? No compromise? It was clear to me that the military was my employer and my personal goals would have to wait.

Putting my personal crisis behind me, I learned good leadership and managerial skills and became extremely proficient in filling out government forms. After several years of carrier operations on the high seas and other eye opening experiences, I was reassigned to the Bureau of Naval Personnel in Arlington, Virginia. Imagine an unmarried young naval officer in our nation's capital where, at that time, the women outnumbered the men eight to one!

I loved the Navy, but the Vietnam War began to escalate. In August of 1965, word came that all naval personnel were going to have their tours of duty extended. I made a decision, a good one at that, to leave the military with an honorable discharge. I lost my health insurance and could not collect unemployment. I did not get a gold watch but was free to pursue my life's ambition if only I knew what that might be. I had served my country well, and was too young and naive to be overly concerned.

I would spend the next 32 years of my life in the Corporate world. I traveled extensively, lived four years in Europe and worked for many different companies

Officially my Corporate career began in late 1965 with Ortho Pharmaceutical Corporation, a subsidiary of Johnson & Johnson. I was trained and developed expertise in the areas of birth control and family planning for women. It was a job I really enjoyed.

Working for Ortho, I was around doctors every day. At one time, when I was around 27, I considered going back to school to study medicine. Even at that time I was wondering whether there was more to life than working as a drug representative, visiting doctors and calling on hospitals and pharmacies daily. The idea of going back to school for more education seemed attractive to me.

However, when I realized how much I would have to sacrifice and how many years it would take and at what cost, the fantasy faded and I lost my nerve. I also reminded myself of my lack-luster performance as an undergraduate and questioned whether I had the drive and ambition to complete medical school.

My undergraduate degree was in business administration. I had very little math, chemistry, biology and had flunked physics. Those subjects were required for admission to medical school. My physician friends indicated that several science courses would be required. This would mean two years of college, no guaranteed admission to medical school and at a cost I was not prepared to pay. It was easy for me to convince myself that I did not have what it takes.

Success does not happen by external combustion and I have had difficulty finding the spark to ignite my internal engine. Besides, I was earning around $30,000 a year and was not in a great hurry to push that income aside. It was an abrupt end to a short-lived fantasy. This experience was the first of many indicators that I was allowing my life to drift

By society's standards, I was successful and was earning good money. The problem was, as I now look back, I was spending all of it. Instant gratification was not fast enough for me. I quickly became an expert in deficit spending. *Charge it! Charge it! Charge it!* was my battle cry. Spending all my money seemed like a good choice. The ripple effect of those choices ultimately became an issue when, now in my fifties, I suddenly became unemployed. I was very upset. I had no plan, no job, no income and no savings for a rainy day. Believe me, it was more like a thunderstorm. As I saw it, I was a victim of a system that lured you in, drained you dry and left you in the end with little or no personal reward. In retrospect, it was not the system. It was me. The blame rested squarely on my shoulders. I had not taken responsibility for the choices I made.

Truthfully, I had been concerned about the lack of stability and satisfaction in many areas of my life for years. I constantly berated myself for not having money in the bank, a secure job, a retirement plan, or an estate to leave my children. Ever since meeting Bonnie, who would later become my wife and was the epitome of hard work, good choices, and very happy with her life, I had been feverishly trying to get another corporate job. My constant courtship with failure was forcing me to jump back into the corporate frying pan that had been burning me up for the last thirty years. While I believed it was my only alternative, my soul, as it turned out, believed otherwise. So did my wife. What did she see in me that I could not see in myself?

Believing a return to Corporate America would be

my only salvation, and in exchange for a hefty fee, I sought help and advice from a well-known career management company. The size of the fee was in inverse proportion to the result. They video tested me, put me through a Meyer Briggs psychological profile, taught me interviewing skills, coached me on how to write an effective resume (I am not convinced there is such a thing) and did all they could to prepare me for my **professional** career search. Following their advice, I dutifully read, among others, *What Color Is Your Parachute?* and *Dress For Success*. I mailed several hundred resumes and made hundreds of unsolicited phone calls, most of which were never returned. I could have wallpapered my bathroom with all the politely written rejection letters. Although it works sometimes, for me, it was a time consuming, frustrating exercise in total futility. Was there a message in all this frustration?

In June of 1995, the door of opportunity seemed to open. I was hired to resuscitate a dying company in Atlanta. Bonnie and I were living together but up to this point had resisted the temptation of marriage. We were in love, but, as Bonnie put it, "Why spoil a good thing?" It was actually at the insistence of our blended family, her kids and mine, that we realized it was commitment time. I was getting tired of being introduced by her parents as… "Bonnie's gentleman friend." On July 16[th,] 1995, we made it official and became husband and wife. It was the best decision I ever made. After seven days in Aruba, we moved to Atlanta on August first.

The job opportunity was doomed from the beginning. Seven months passed and the wealthy owner threw in the towel. The company was sold and once again I was out of work. There was no severance pay and I never got the professional courtesy of a telephone call from my employer.

It was a knockout punch, and I hit the canvas. My character was bloodied and my self-esteem was on the floor. I lost all remaining confidence and had serious doubts as to my self worth. I wanted to believe that I had made a difference, but if I died today what would people say? I did not have an answer. I believed my children would have nothing to be proud of in their Dad, nothing they could really look up to and identify with. I would leave no estate, no money and no legacy.

By this time I was desperate. The *gold watch* became the symbol of my lack of significance—the sum total of my achievements after thirty-five years of corporate loyalty and expectation. Of course, I never got the gold watch and, frankly, it is not important. I have known individuals who dedicated their entire lives to their jobs and all they got in return, if they were lucky, was a pat on the back. There had to be more to life. The *gold watch* simply became the symbol of my search for respect and recognition.

Having adopted the *gold watch* as representing my disappointment in Corporate America, I decided the only way I could get back at the system was to write a book about it. My real reason was simply to vent my anger, but I did not know it at the time. I was in denial. The book was to be called—yes, you guessed it: *Where's Your Gold Watch?*

I was so certain about my mission for this book and the title I had chosen, I prematurely had business cards, bookmarks, and other promotional materials printed.

The irony is that my initial intention in writing turned out to be the stimulus for a dramatic change in my life. I experienced a shift in attitude that was one hundred and eighty degrees opposite to that which motivated me in the first place.

For example, I learned that my frustration and disappointment was not really toward Corporate America, but towards myself. I also realized that everything I had done in my life up to this point was essential in bringing me to where I am today.

As I examined my life during the process of writing this book, my frustrations dissipated and my disappointments began to disappear. The need to write *Where's Your Gold Watch?* as an expression of my anger also disappeared. Just as the nature of the book changed, so did its title. The new title became *Kiss Yourself Hello!*

6

MARRIAGE MATTERS

"Anger is just one letter away from Danger"

Unknown

Having found up to this point little substance in my professional life to inform me as to who the real Phil Parker was, I looked back to my first marriage for clues and lessons I might have learned during the sixteen years it lasted.

What began as a questionable marriage ended in a nasty divorce! A Failure? Why? Perhaps the only thing my first wife and I had in common was that we got married on the same day.

Marriage, as most of us veterans know well, is the continuous process of getting used to things we do not expect. Comedian Bill Cosby said, "Two people living together, day after day, may be the one miracle the Vatican overlooked." I quickly learned that two of the great myths in the world are that marriage is forever and life is easy.

If love is blind then marriage is certainly the eye opener. Looking back on my marriage is no less depressing than was the marriage itself.

I was thirty years old when I got married for the first time. Supposedly, I was a mature, intelligent young man who was through sowing and harvesting his wild oats and ready to settle down. From the beginning it was a disastrous partnership and remained that way for its' duration.

We were two individuals who came from two different worlds. Mine was a world of trust, love of family, genuine caring for others, and sharing my abundance. From my perspective, hers was a world of contempt, scorn, conflict, mistrust, anger, and self-righteousness. It was never one of partnership but rather one of two people of the opposite sex conveniently living under the same roof. Conversations were brief and limited in scope. There was rarely any discussion and little humor.

We could not have been more opposite in our thought process. I perceived myself as easy-going and very accommodating while she always had a *her way or the highway* attitude. Rather than creating a marriage of balance, it was a case of opposites attracted to each other to create a marriage of chaos. It was like touching the negative and positive ends of jumper cables together while still connected to the battery. Sparks were flying everywhere at all times!

In the legal sense, the marriage survived for sixteen years. During those years I harbored feelings of anger and frustration. I had endured constant verbal and mental abuse. It was not until my second marriage that I began to realize just how much of my own sense of value and self-esteem I had lost.

It is painful to look back on those years. It brought back many unpleasant memories such as sitting down with my children, and telling them their mother and I were getting divorced. They were thirteen and eleven at the time. It was a time of turmoil, confusion and much pain in my life. Was I a failure as a father? Had I abandoned my kids? Did the failure of my marriage show weakness, or did it show recognizable strength in moving on with my life? Notice I said **my** failure in **my** marriage. That was my perception then. I know now that it was just as much my wife's failure at marriage as it was mine. I previously failed to see it in that light.

Our children represented the only positive element in the relationship. They were the reason I remained in the marriage as long as I did. I found warmth and safety under a quilt of guilt. I was ashamed and scared. I felt awful and endured many nights with a churning stomach and tears that flowed without restraint. How could I leave them? Would I become a deadbeat dad? Would they still love me? Could I bear not to see them on a regular basis? Would I be able to afford the alimony and child support? Was the breakup of my marriage my fault and was I trying hard enough to save the marriage? How would I explain the divorce to my family and friends? What would I do with the rest of my life?

As always, there were no comfortable answers. There was no easy solution. I had to deal with the reality that our marriage was never going to succeed. I lamented that I had *wasted* sixteen years of my life trying to please someone whom I could not satisfy. In fact, I now realize that we could not satisfy each other.

Until recently, that was my perception of the situation. For years I viewed my divorce as one of the biggest failures in my life. It was a painful experience to my ego and my wallet. No man can appreciate just how short a month can be until he has to pay alimony and child support. On my behalf, I was never late with a payment.

As I approach my 60th birthday, I am beginning to acknowledge and confront the anger and rage suppressed during my first marriage and the scar it left. It has been my silent companion since my divorce in 1984. I used to believe I harbored no anger. Today, I know better. I am only now recalling the yelling, the cursing, the tension, and my loss of control.

During the break up of my marriage, I vented my anger on several occasions. Once, after dropping off my children at their house, I was sitting in my car in my wife's driveway. I rolled down my window for what I thought would be a civil conversation but which turned into a nasty confrontation with my soon to be ex-wife. I was furious and can vividly remember clenching my teeth, tightening my fists and screaming obscenities at the top of my lungs, vowing that I would never speak to *that woman* again. It was not a pretty scene. On a scale of one to ten, I judged it as UGLY. I felt deeply ashamed of my outburst. I promised myself I would not do that again. It was the tip of the iceberg. Years later I recognized venting my anger was the healthiest thing I could have done for myself. It is a slow and continuous process but each day I am flushing out the acid of anger and lightening the burden of bitterness.

Was my divorce really a total failure in my life – something to feel ashamed of? Until recently, I could not see it any other way. Now I see there were valuable lessons learned from that experience. I get to see how I made choices in my life and how they have led me to where I am today. There is a positive and negative outcome in every adversity and every choice we make has its own ripple effect, good or bad, and offers an opportunity to learn. Whether we seize that opportunity or not is simply another choice we make.

Eleven years passed before I married again. Honestly, I never expected to re-marry but often life has a way of taking over.

Today, approaching the fourth year of my second marriage, I no longer question my own self-worth and confidence. As I look back, I have come to the conclusion that my first marriage was simply a trial heat for the main event. I practiced, paid a price, but learned well. Now I am married to my best friend, my confidant, my lover and my consummate support system. I have found my soulmate. I am the happy, contented and loved husband of Bonnie Ross-Parker.

7

NO ANSWERS   MORE QUESTIONS

**"It is not enough for me to ask questions;
I want to know how to answer the one
question that seems to encompass
everything I face: What am I here for?"**

Abraham J. Heschel

Disappointingly, I found that for me my introspection and soul searching created more questions. For example:

- **What had I accomplished in my life that was meaningful?**
- **What was my purpose on this planet?**
- **How much of a difference, if any, had I made in other people's lives?**

As you may imagine, in my confused state, it was difficult to find any positive responses to these questions. My mind had been conditioned to search for the negative.

Take a good look at your life! Are you happy? Is it fulfilling? Are you doing what you want to do? Are you materially wealthy but spiritually poor?

Check out your relationships! Are they working? Are they giving you what you want and need?

Examine your marriage! Are you growing together or dying together?

Look at your economic well being! Are you living from paycheck to paycheck? Are you drowning in credit card debt? Are you simply exchanging hours for dollars? Are you following the 40/40/40 Plan? You know, working 40 hours a week for 40 years expecting to retire on 40 percent of your income.

Is your life in balance? Do you want the lifestyle you have? Do you have the lifestyle you deserve? Do you deserve the lifestyle you want?

As you may imagine, at first it was difficult to find any positive responses to these questions. Initially my mind had been conditioned to feast on the negative and fast on the positive. It seems to be a mindset many of us embrace. Complaining about the noise when opportunity knocks is a benign example of our conditioning but illustrative of the process.

The initial exhilaration of my walk in the neighborhood had all but disappeared. Searching for the meaning in my past had really produced nothing but a sense of worthlessness and depression. I was as low as I have ever been in my life. Thinking about it now, I realize that it was the dark night of my soul.   My pipe had gone out!

PERSONAL REFLECTIONS

8

SCRAPING MYSELF OFF THE ROAD

"If you fall down, land on your back because if you can look up, you can get up."

Les Brown

After my cosmic kick and all the soul searching, I remained depressed for a long period of time. I wallowed in self-pity and self-criticism. During that entire period, I berated myself for my bad decisions and poor choices. I highlighted my mistakes, emphasized my shortcomings and agonized over the unrecognized opportunities I let slip by.

Privately, I withdrew into my personal cave and sulked. At the same time, I chastised myself unmercifully and continued to question my own significance.

It was early in 1997, almost eight months after that walk in the neighborhood, that I began to drag myself out of the pit. The first thing to hit me was a realization that I was now living with an angel – a woman who understood who I was and loved me unconditionally. I had never known what it felt like to come home to a loving, supportive, nurturing and caring woman. As I struggled with my own sense of self-worth, Bonnie was accessible to share in my struggle. Through our many and lengthy discussions, it became more and more obvious how much she cared. I was grateful for her support and for the space she gave me to arrive at my own solutions. I was accepted for who I was rather than for my public persona. She recognized my lack of self-confidence and my insecurities but remained non-judgmental. My wife became my best friend. Our relationship strengthens each day. I am a fortunate man. My friend, and fellow author and speaker Willie Jolley would say, "I'm truly blessed and highly favored."

I began to talk more freely and for the first time spoke honestly with Bonnie about what was happening to me and how I was feeling. Of course, it came as no surprise to her. She had witnessed my withdrawal and was anxiously waiting for me to emerge from my cocoon. I was a lot more transparent to her than I was to myself.

As my depression began to loosen its grip, we began to talk for hours at a time. Slowly I shared everything with her – my disappointments and my failures.

The lingering pain I was feeling from my first marriage began to pour out. It was time to face the music, get a new conductor, re-write the lyrics and move on with life. I had to make better choices and initiate positive changes.

I realize now how important it was to share my pain with someone who was a close observer, non-judgmental and who loved me enough to listen. This was the first step in my healing. My willingness to be honest was a major breakthrough.

I still did not know what course I wanted to follow. I was certain I did not want to return to the nine-to-five corporate world. What **would** I do? What **could** I do? More importantly, what did I **want** to do? Once again, Bonnie would be the one to help me.

PERSONAL REFLECTIONS

9

PASSION UNCOVERED

"Only passions, great passions, can elevate the soul to do great things."

Denis Diderot, French Philosopher

It was obvious that Bonnie wanted me to take action. She was unhappy with my indecision and wondered how long it would take me to get my act together. Finally, one evening as I was stretched out on the couch, Bonnie asked me two significant questions. "What do you want to do?" and "What makes you happiest?"

"Public speaking," I said, without a moment's hesitation. " My passion is public speaking. I love talking to audiences and telling stories."

I was shocked at how quickly I responded. It was almost as if someone else had spoken. Bonnie and I talked more and agreed that public speaking was not only my passion, but that I was good at it.

She convinced me that I had a powerful story to

tell and the talent to do it. It amazed me how much faith she had in my abilities. She went on to say that I was a great storyteller and why not consider writing a book.

After much discussion back and forth, I was beginning to accept my own talent – at least the public speaking aspect of it. I was not sure about the idea of writing a book. Nevertheless, I began to feel energized. I even came up with a title. I would call it *Where's Your Gold Watch?*

By that time, it was getting late and we were both exhausted, so the conversation was put on hold. That night after we had retired, I laid in bed thinking about the exciting possibility of writing a book and the old negativity began to return. I questioned the validity of writing a book, especially one that was largely about me. As far as I was concerned, writing a book about my life did not seem like anything I wanted to do. I could not believe anyone would want to read anything I might write. It was like the old Groucho Marx quote, "I wouldn't want to be a member of a club that would have me as a member." It was evident how my processes, my negative attitude and my self-perception had sculpted my life. My self-esteem and confidence were still below water level. I had to learn to get out of my own way.

10

PURPOSE   DISCOVERED

**"Thoughts lead on to purposes;
purposes go forth in action;
actions form habits; habits decide character;
and character fixes our destiny."**

Tyron Edwards

I began spending a lot of time at a bookstore in my neighborhood. It was like having my own office and the rent wasn't bad either. I'd get my coffee, butter a bagel, and select a book. If I didn't like my selection, I'd put it back on the shelf and choose another. No one seemed to object to my daily habit as long as I bought an occasional cup of coffee and other goodies. The staff was friendly, very helpful, and I got to know them well.

I immersed myself in the self-development and self-empowerment section. What an eye opener! Slowly my life started to make sense.   I began to see how I had created my life by my thoughts, my attitudes, my choices and my perceptions.   It was equivalent to pouring ice water on my brain. What a revelation!

The soul-searching started to pay off. I was un-covering the truth about myself. I asked myself some of life's most basic questions: *What's life all about? What's really important to me, and what do I care most about? Has my life had a real impact on anyone? What legacy will I leave my children?* The questions came a lot easier then the answers. As I continue to read, I am beginning to find some answers. Not all the answers came directly from books. However, reading helped plow the fertile garden of my mind and enabled me to find many of my own answers.

For example, I began to recognize my *fear of failure.* I have many talents, skills and life experiences that make me an interesting person. People enjoy being in my company and listening to my stories. The one recurring thought that became clear to me was that I wanted my journey, my experiences and my setbacks to serve as a beacon of hope to others who have had similar life struggles.

One day my daughter called from Dallas. She had volunteered my services as a speaker to the company where she was employed.   That company was

GeicoDirect. After some discussion with GEICO, I agreed to do two one-hour motivational speeches to a large number of their telephone sales force.

For the first time in my life I experienced the feeling of being *in the zone*. In my heart I knew I could give the speech and do it well. I had done well as a speaker in Corporate America and I was skilled at telling stories and making people laugh. What an exhilarating thought.

My busy self-doubting mind kept asking what I would speak about. What pearls of wisdom did I have to offer several hundred insurance agents? What would I talk about that could make a significant difference in their lives?

As I have already shared, for much of my life I have focused on the negative and had seen things from that point of view. I felt I had been dealt a weak hand; that things rarely worked out for me and the corporate world had betrayed me. At this point in my life, it was clear that I needed to correct the gyroscope of my attitude. On the premise that you teach what you most need to learn, I made ***attitude*** the topic of my presentation.

The time had come. I could feel my heart racing in anticipation. My knees were moving rapidly in concert toward each other, and my stomach felt like a twisted pretzel. I was nervous but had prepared well and my

nervousness quickly disappeared. I immediately connected with my audience. My daughter was in the front
row. I had a great sense of excitement and pride.

I was a huge success. A standing ovation rein-
forced what I already knew. I had taken a big step in my
journey to become a motivational speaker. I had searched
my soul and found both my purpose and passion.

11

We Teach What We Most Need To Learn

"To teach is to learn twice over."

Joseph Joubert

For the first time in my life I was willing to recognize and appreciate the positive forces in my life. I knew that not only did I need to talk about a good attitude but I also had to project one as well. To facilitate my attitude adjustment and help me develop my presentation skills, I sought access to world class motivational speakers, trainers, and coaches.

In November of 1995, I was introduced to The Peoples Network. TPN, as it is called, is a digital satellite TV channel that provides programs focusing exclusively on professional and personal development in all aspects of your life. Referred to as the *Success Channel*, it is the only television channel of its kind in the world. Its faculty are the **Who's Who** of business and personal development such as Brian Tracy, Les Brown, Jim Rohn, Mark Victor Hanson, Nido Qubein, Dr. Bernie

Siegal, Michael Gerber, George Frazier and others. This channel provides me with a resource perfect for my work. TPN began to help crystallize my thoughts with a daily diet of motivation, business strategies and inspiration as I continued to re-engineer my life.

Spending more and more time at the bookstore, I selected books that covered similar topics. I even began to read some of the more spiritually oriented material like M. Scott Peck's *A Road Less Traveled*, *Conversations With God*, by Neale Donald Walsch, and *The Mutant Message Down Under*, by Marla Morgan. These books opened up my mind, excited my spirit and touched my heart.

The idea that we *teach best what we most need to learn*, has special significance for me. It gives me permission to go on learning and developing the speaking career I have chosen. Whenever I get down on myself and wonder, *who are you to be telling other people how they should live?*, I remind myself of this statement. I was ready to learn and eager to teach.

I know that by encouraging others to ask the same questions of themselves as those I have asked of myself, I may help move them forward . I hope by sharing my own experiences, I will illuminate the way for others and help them make more sense out of what is happening in their lives.

Having unilaterally labeled myself as a failure, I would now be able to talk to people who have judged themselves as harshly as I had judged myself. My experiences coupled with my personal journey would be the bases on which to share my insights. I could now speak from the experience of my own misconception. My mission was to help people become accepting of themselves irrespective of their outer circumstances.

Slowly I began to realize that this new career was the key to regaining my confidence and crucial to my own healing. In order to become a professional speaker, I was going back to school to re-make myself.

PERSONAL REFLECTIONS

12

HAVING FUN AT AGE 59

**"Growing old is no more than a bad habit
which a busy man has no time to form."**

Andre Maurois

As I began to share and talk about my years of trading hours for dollars in Corporate America, I continued to use humor as a vehicle to get my message across to my audiences. I dropped the self-deprecating stuff. I now know that you get what you affirm! Sharing the error of my ways, I hoped to inspire them to re-create themselves not only as successful people but also as individuals truly in touch with who they are and where they are going. In other words, my focus is to help people balance their lives. This would be the focus of a speech entitled, *Life's a Business, So Let's Get Busy.*

My confidence increased and the frustration about my past lost its edge. I could easily identify with my audiences because I knew that many of them had also experienced similar feelings and challenges in their own lives. The irony, which I did not see at the time, is that I am a good speaker and communicator precisely because I had lived my life as a gatherer of information rather than a provider of information. Having successfully created myself as a failure in my journey through life, I am now able to speak to people from the experience of those wounds.

As a speaker, I began to realize the power of my message could be found in my wounds while the strength of the message was in my own vulnerability. When I poked fun at my own merry-go-round life, those who heard me speak began to understand its futility. My audiences knew I paid a high tuition for my experiences thus making my insights more meaningful. I was confident I would become a skilled communicator and better motivator precisely because I had spent my life in the opposite polarity.

If I, at the ripening age of fifty-nine, could take risks, learn new skills, make better choices and begin a new and rewarding career, so could anyone. After much soul searching, I am getting comfortable with the notion that life will support me as long as I do not resist it, will reward me when I trust it and abundance will follow. As

I continuously struggle to move beyond my comfort zone, take responsibility for my choices and better manage life's risks, I am beginning to create significance in my life. Moulding my new career armed with a new set of positive attitudes, I am making my life purposeful and passionate. I am flowing with life rather than fighting with life. I am taking control of the business of my life. **You can do the same!**

PERSONAL REFLECTIONS

PART TWO

TRANSITIONS

The essence of being human
is the capacity to desire
personal growth and
the will to change.
Through the agony of failure
we learn to fly and
then to soar to
unexpected heights.

13

MIRROR   MIRROR

**"Our environment, the world
in which we live and work,
is a mirror of our
attitudes and expectations."**

Earl Nightingale

If you are still here after accompanying me on my journey of self-discovery in Part One, the chances are that you found something of yourself in my story.

- Maybe you, like me, have spent a large part of your life trying in vain to find recognition through outward success and the accumulation of wealth, while remaining inwardly unfulfilled.
- Perhaps you are at that point of trying to justify your existence and searching for your significance in the world in ways other than material success.
- Maybe you woke up one morning, looked in your rear view mirror and began asking the

same kinds of questions I asked myself at age fifty-six, when I woke up and realized how I had spent almost thirty five years of my life.

- Perhaps you are asking, "Where am I going?" or "What's my plan for the rest of my life? Do I have a plan or am I following someone else's plan?"

- You, too, may be wondering, "If my life ended at this moment, what legacy would I leave my family, friends and society?

**If any of this is true for you, hang in with me.
It will be illuminating!**

Before that evening stroll in the neighborhood, I used to notice only people who hated their jobs, constantly complained about the weather, the traffic, the government and anything else that was not to their liking. It seemed to me that everyone was either in a bad relationship or lonely because they did not have a relationship; living from paycheck to paycheck; upset with the I.R.S; did not like the car they were driving; broke; not being paid their worth; and generally miserable because they had no time to have fun. I saw people leading very stressful and unproductive lives without purpose or passion.

Then it **HIT** me!   I was actually looking at myself in the mirror.

At an early age, I learned to live by other people's rules in order to please them so I could get what I wanted. I did it for over fifty years because it was easy and became habitual. I did not have to think or establish rules of my own. I also learned to be critical and to sift and sort for the negative.   That way, by blaming others for my lack of success, I could feel better about myself.

WARNING: If you recognize any of this in yourself, **PLEASE** avoid the temptation to criticize yourself or beat yourself up for being who you are – no matter how bad you think you are. ***The key to making changes that will lead to being a great deal happier is that you must begin from a place of deep acceptance of where you are right now.***   It is vital to have compassion for yourself, recognizing that if life has not been easy you have done the very best you could. You need to accept that many of the things that have happened along the way in the drama of your life were divinely guided and happened for a reason. They were lessons you needed to learn in order to make you stronger, wiser, more compassionate, more generous, and so on. Judging yourself or your circumstances is therefore futile and self-defeating and it will keep you stuck right where you are in your own unhappiness.

Earl Nightingale once said, *You become what you think about.* I think it goes further than that. Your whole world reflects how you think. Life itself mirrors back to you precisely what you think and believe. Your world is indeed a projection of self, a conscious expression of your subconscious mind.

I saw the world as negative and unfriendly because I filtered everything I saw through my own lens colored with negative beliefs, attitudes and patterns of thinking. I projected negativity onto the big screen of my life and the picture was seriously out of focus.

Guess what I got back? Negativity! Guess why my first marriage was to a woman who knowingly or unknowingly fed me *a-la-carte negativity* on a daily basis? Guess why I was upset at the corporate world?

Had I formed a solid belief system early in my life that I was OK, and did not have to do things I did not want to do in order to be loved, I would have been describing the world to you in quite a different way. In short, I would have had a more positive outlook.

It is not that either outlook is truer than the other. Both are equally true (or untrue), because life is always pretty much how we see it. Life is *always* a matter of perception. Our minds do not distinguish between reality and perception. This is a crucial point – and a very exciting one too, because it means that at any moment, you can **CHOOSE** how to see your life. We see this expressed in its simplest form when we say that we can choose to see the glass as half empty or half full. It is equally true to say that we can choose to see a diagnosis of a life threatening disease either as a tragedy or as a challenge and opportunity to learn what healing is all about.

PAUSE AND PONDER:

What is the state of your world?

What is the thought pattern – the color of your lens?

How are you consciously choosing your focus?

PERSONAL REFLECTIONS

14

COMFORTABLE COFFINS

**"Most people would rather be
comfortable than competent."**

Nido Qubein

The extent to which we experience life from a place of fear, also defines our perception of life. If we are frightened by change, worried about security, protective of everything we have lest we might lose it and so on, we will live rigid and unfulfilled lives. By choosing the safe road, avoiding risk, moving little, changing seldom and buying a lot of insurance, we are held captive in the prison of our minds. Let me share with you a personal example.

In January, 1989, I returned to the Washington, D.C. area after spending almost five years in Germany. Through mutual friends, I reconnected with Bonnie Ross, a woman I had not seen in 14 years. Each of our first marriages had ended and as we began spending time together, we began sharing a comfortable and intimate relationship. I was enjoying the honesty, the trust, the caring, and certainly the intimacy. It was wonderful and exciting. Bonded by our past history, I knew her parents and her children; we grew closer.

Suddenly, I got nervous. I was scared and uncertain of my feelings. Our relationship was happening too fast for me and I did not want to risk giving up the freedom of being a bachelor. I panicked. I decided to move.

Packing everything I owned into my car, I drove 645 miles south to Atlanta, Georgia, where I had lived before moving to Germany. Atlanta spelled *SAFETY*! My daughter was attending the University of Georgia and my good friend Peter was living close by. I could return to the same barber that had cut my hair from 1977 through 1984. I was back in familiar surroundings. I was safely encased in my comfort zone. I found a job and for the next 18 months I worked, worked out and spent many evening hours on the phone with the woman I left behind.

I was a slow learner. It finally hit me! I was in love. I guess it took me those many months of being in separate cities to realize the risk was not losing my freedom. The real risk was losing the woman with whom I wanted to spend the rest of my life.

I called her and for the first time expressed my love. That call created the turning point in our relationship as we both said *yes* to spending the rest of our lives together. Bonnie agreed to fly to Atlanta. On November 11, 1991 we packed up my car and drove 645 miles north returning to her home in Potomac, Maryland. We continued nurturing our relationship and creating the lifestyle we enjoy today.

The relentless pursuit of comfort as the prime goal in our lives is actually a form of slow death. The ultimate risk-free, comfortable environment occurs when we are lying in our coffin. Many people spend a great proportion of their life in a virtual coffin – just waiting for the real one to show up. Too many people die around the age of twenty-five and just wait until they are around seventy-five before they actually get buried.

To really feel alive, in the full sense of being alive-- not just semi-conscious as I was-- we must push through our fears, take risks and move boldly into the unknown. We must try new things, leap out of our comfort zones and trust in God – who, by the way, never makes mistakes! We must not expect perfection but rather strive for excellence. Only God is perfect!

Life itself is the ultimate risk. You can not cheat it and you can not beat it. We are all born. We will all die.

Everything in between is negotiable. You can not leave it alive. But there is a big difference between being a risk taker and simply taking risks. A risk taker manages risk, knowing the extent of it in advance, preparing for it well, and asking for divine assistance. Mountain climbers are risk takers. They survive because they prepare for the mountain, respect the mountain and follow strict safety procedures. They become experts at managing their risks.

Emotional risk is another form of risk that few people are willing to take. I was one of them. I would not have owned up to it before my *experience*. I saw myself as an open, caring and sharing person. If you wanted to know anything about Phil Parker, you just had to ask, I thought. Wearing my emotions and sharing my feelings were, I convinced myself, easy for me. To this day I find myself teary-eyed when watching a poignant love story, attending weddings, bar mitzvahs, or listening to the National Anthem. Yet, I was constantly reading and hearing about macho men who were emotionless, thoughtless, addicted to TV, and less caring than women. They would prefer a high-tech remote control rather than a meaningful relationship. I did not put myself in that category.

Now I realize just how much I avoided my own emotions and made sure I protected my vulnerability.

Sure, I would tell you all you needed to know about Phil Parker, as long as you stayed away from anything that might require me to reveal my authentic self under the masks that I hid behind. I was not even aware of my many disguises. How about you?

Have you ever risked your own vulnerability?

PAUSE AND PONDER:

How comfortable is your life?

What kinds of risks do you take and how do you manage them?

How do you embrace change?

What is the most significant change you have experienced during the last twelve months?

PERSONAL REFLECTIONS

15

LIFE IN REVERSE

"The art of life is not *controlling* what happens to us but, *using* what happens to us."

Gloria Steinhem

When I began this life-review process and looked at who I really was behind the masks, I realized I was not only protecting my emotional vulnerability, but also very resistant to change and risk. Held prisoner by mental handcuffs and inaccurate in the assessment of my own vulnerability, I was in denial about my fears, my inadequacies and lack of self-confidence. I was rigid in my thought process. I was reluctant to step out of my comfort zone into a world of risks, changing values and high expectations.

By refusing to acknowledge all of the above, I was not being honest with myself. I believed Phil Parker had has act together. I lied to myself. Do you?

I was ambitiously lazy and over the years had

worked hard at doing nothing. I had cultivated a habit of resting before I got tired. It has been a difficult habit to break. Granted, I had worked consistently for thirty five years earning a respectable living. But, I have often wondered why I was not earning more. I accomplished financial freedom only once in my life while I was living and working in Germany. From 1984 through 1989, as an American working in Europe under a United States government contract, I was able to enjoy tax-free status on the first seventy thousand dollars of income.

Was it my poor choice of jobs, lack of proper skills, no opportunity, or just bad luck? What was my problem? Finally, my neon light switched on! I had never accepted responsibility for my own failures.

PAUSE AND PONDER:

> **What responsibility do you accept for your choices?**
> **How much time do you waste on activity instead of productivity?**

I am uncomfortable confessing to the number of companies that employed me. The list follows:

Ortho Pharmaceutical Corporation
RCA Corporation
Univac
Evergreen Computers
Ampex Corporation
Perkin-Elmer
Data Printer
Hazeltine Corporation
Applied Digital Data Systems
CIE Terminals
SMS Data Products
Novell
C3, Inc.
Mail Boxes Etc.
AmeriVap Systems
Heel Quik!

The last eight opportunities were during a thirteen-year period.

Many of these opportunities were challenging and rewarding. Others were job changes either for a larger salary, relocation, or corporate politics. It was obvious I had no defined career path but rather a hodge-podge of jobs spanning a lengthy period of my life. I was simply showing up to collect a paycheck.

I admit it. I never assumed any responsibility for my career. *Who is taking responsibility for your career?* Helen Hayes, the great stage and screen actress, once said, "Every human being is born under a great tragedy and it isn't the original sin. We're born with the tragedy of having to grow up. Most of us don't have the courage to do so." Sometimes, I am still not convinced I've grown up. How about you?

I was without goals. *Live for today and let tomorrow take care of itself* was my motto. My dreams never put on work clothes. My life was a perpetual revolving door. I never knew if I was entering or exiting. I existed without purpose or passion. I had no plan for my career, my legacy, or my life. Enjoying a *get high* philosophy of living, I was a master of the quick fix. I was content to do whatever made me happy at the time. One day, I am not exactly sure when, God's plan took over. It was called **LIFE!**

Little by little, my horizon seemed to clear. Whereas I once had no vision of where I wanted to go, I was beginning to find some direction. The compass of my life was emerging, and it was pointing forward.

Until that time, I was living my life in reverse. I wanted more things and more money so I could do more of what I thought would make me happy. I was obsessed about my lack of success, beat myself up unmercifully for not having a huge bank account and spent most of my time feeling depressed. As I began to accept true happiness comes from within rather than without, my life began to change.

Happiness cannot be purchased at your local mall. It cannot be prescribed from your primary care physician. Like a precious gem, it must be discovered in the mind of your soul. To find my happiness, I had to decide what was important to me and follow my path.

It took time and patience before I began to understand that to find happiness, I had to be honest with myself, peel off all my masks and look deeply into the mirror of my spirit. Only when I was able to listen to my heart was I able to move forward, discover my passion and achieve personal satisfaction.

Fill the cubicles of your mind with purpose, passion, commitment, enthusiasm and humor. Recognize opportunity in adversity, take risks, and open up the panoramic vista of your mind to change. Give yourself permission to *let go* of the past and focus on the present. Be a witness to the progress of change. Welcome it. Create a conscious awareness of it. Accept no limitations. Ask yourself, ***How*** *did I change today?* and, ***What*** *did I* *change today?*   Break through your mental ceiling and never let your thoughts be so narrow that you can see through a keyhole with both eyes.

If you are not traveling in a direction you like, it is time to get your hands dirty and clean up your life. First accept what life has given you. Then shape it into whatever you want it to be. Revolutionize your mind by refurbishing your thoughts. Clean out the closet of your past! Get rid of old baggage!

I began the process in late 1995. Let me share some examples of what I did to facilitate change in my life.

I surrounded myself with people who were positive, enthusiastic and had high energy levels. I began to value my time, not wasting it on activities that did not move me in the direction I wanted to go. I asked for help. As a speaker, I looked to the National Speakers Association for assistance. As an author, I talked to other authors. I found a mentor with similar interests. I found that people are willing to help those who are clear in what they want to accomplish. I read and researched sources for information and ideas.

Living a life of contented complacency, I had no long-term goals and dreams. I did not even have a short-term plan. I was nourished by the crumbs that life threw my way--some good, some bad. There were some bugs on the windshield of my life. The untimely loss of my parents and the demise of my first marriage caused me pain and anguish. Is it possible I had to face each of those challenges to move me to where I am in my life today? I had not experienced any tragedy in my life. Of course, I did not experience much personal growth either. That did not seem to matter. Avoidance had become my best companion. Avoiding conflict, skirting important decisions and denying my own insecurities made me feel better for the moment but crescendoed into much stress and anxiety over the years.

To be happy, we must get in touch with our real selves and look honestly and deeply into our own souls to uncover our passions and the obstacles we erect that keep us from doing what we love. Identifying and removing those obstacles is what re-engineering our life is all about. It is what self-development is all about. It is what therapy is all about. It is what this book is about.

How you choose to remove those obstacles is up to you, but remove them you must. Genuine forgiveness and letting go of the past is a key part of the process. You cannot get to a place of peace if you are inwardly at war, holding on to resentments and pain.

PAUSE AND PONDER:

Stop being a victim or seeing yourself as a victim.

Take responsibility.

Empty your hands of past choices.

For more on this, I recommend you read Caroline Myss's book, *Why People Don't Heal, and How They Can*.

Once you have begun the process of removing the emotional and mental stumbling blocks that have caused you to have negative and self-defeating thought patterns and beliefs, you will move forward to pursue your passion and find happiness. This will not happen by waving a magic wand, but through small steps of progress toward self-discovery. It requires intimate honesty. Only when you identify those areas that are holding you back from living a purposeful life will you be able to implement change. If you are in a stressfull relationship, **ADMIT IT!** If you drink too much, **ADMIT IT!** If you do not spend enough quality time with your family, **ADMIT IT!** If you watch too much TV, **ADMIT IT!** If you are overweight and do not take care of your health, **ADMIT IT!** If you always procrastinate, **ADMIT IT!** You must take ownership of whatever it is that is holding you back if you want to create a better future.

There is an old Chinese Proverb that says, "*Make your first 500 mistakes as fast as you can*". I am certain as I approach my sixtieth birthday, I have seen the effects of my past choices and have made many mistakes. I am now launching the next phase of my life as an author and professional speaker--an opportunity I would not have thought possible a few short years ago.

I am now enthusiastically engaged in the process of discovering who I am. It has been an eerie, energizing, and evolving experience. It has caused me to explore my soul. I am revisiting my past, studying my present and consciously creating my future. That is both bad news and good news. The bad news is that I am not as young as I once was, but the good news is that I am not as old as I am going to get. I have embarked on a wonderful and exciting journey in search of my legacy, my significance, i.e. my **life**style.

PERSONAL REFLECTIONS

16

MISMATCHED, MISGUIDED AND MISPLACED

**"Life is like a garment we
continually try to alter
but which never seems to fit."**

Unknown

There is a Buddhist proverb that says, *"If you don't know where you're going, any path will take you."* Somewhere there is a trail leading to wherever you want to go. You just need to find it and give yourself permission to begin the journey. More often than not, the trail is difficult to find. It was for me. It seems as though my trail was overgrown with problems, crisis, fears, time constraints, anxieties, cynicism, and vindictiveness. Much of the trail was hidden by frustration, anger, and regret. To clear the pathway and reach the quality of life you desire and deserve, you must become skilled at using your mind like a machete. According to Earl Nightingale, *"The quality of your life as well as the direction of your life will be determined by the loftiness of your thoughts and the impact of your actions."*

You will recall from my story in Part 1, that I had no idea what my life's passion was until I went through the pains of revelation. I took a close look at me and began being truthful with myself. I had to discard all of my baggage about being a failure and stop thinking about becoming successful in the corporate world. I faced the fact that I did not want to be a salesman or a business executive. I wanted to be a speaker.

Although I had become unhappy with Corporate America, in truth there never was anything to be unhappy about. The only thing wrong was that I did not fit! I was the proverbial square peg in a round hole. I was filled with frustration and resentment.

It was exactly the same with my first marriage. There was nothing inherently wrong with myself or my wife. It just was not a fit – exactly like my career. Instead of taking responsibility for my own life, and making decisions that would right those situations, I blamed everybody else and sat around envying other people. I then projected a lot of anger at my first wife and adopted the *Gold Watch* as the symbol of my disillusionment with

Corporate America.

Upon reflection, had it not been for the mental abusiveness of my first wife, I probably would not have exited from that marriage and would still be trying to hammer myself into a corporate round hole. Wow, in retrospect, my first marriage was a gift! I did not get a divorce but rather had a divorce experience. I shall be forever grateful. That experience was a good primer and prepared me well.

Having finally found my proper fit, I actually enjoy going back to Corporate America, not as an employee, but as a speaker. I am not carrying any old corporate baggage. I realize that Corporate America is not an entity, or even an institution. It is simply a network of people trying to get along and create value. They need clarity. If, through my speaking, I can help just one person find happiness, one small group define its mission, or one corporation define its identity, I will have succeeded in expressing something of my true self.

Now that I am continually engaged in the process of discovering who I am, I have a deepening appreciation for life. I know that I may not be able to change circumstances but I accept responsibility for the effects those circumstances have on my life. I am more relaxed and having a lot more fun while pursuing the journey toward my own significance. It has been a gradual evolution aided by a lot of introspection. I am constantly revisiting my past for lessons learned, studying my present for opportunities, and consciously creating my future through good choices and positive actions.

PAUSE AND PONDER:

Do you have a handle on who you really are?

What are your greatest strengths and what passion of yours can best use them?

Do you work harder at changing yourself than changing your circumstances?

17

DISCOVERY OF SELF

**"Self-revelation is a cruel process.
The real picture, the real 'you'
never emerges.   Looking for it is as
bewildering as trying to know
how you really look."**

Shashi Deshpande

It seems to me that most of us spend our entire lives trying to justify our existence while searching for our identity. Unable to face the reality of who and what we are, we become more concerned with our image rather than our substance. I was no different. I had learned from my father to project the image but I am now learning to work on my substance. Looking in the mirror, I reveled in the perception of myself rather than the reality of whom others perceived me to be.

During the last several years, there has been much

written about re-engineering the corporation but little written about re-engineering our lives. I knew the time had come for me to do an audit of my life. You might consider doing the same. Searching for the significance of your own existence can be very eye-opening. It was for me. At age fifty-six, I took a look in the rear view mirror of my life, recognized the roller coaster ride I was on, and, not surprisingly, discovered an unfulfilling journey. Waking up one morning, after much personal scrutiny, I faced the realization and painful truth of what I had done with almost thirty-five years of my life. My life had no mission statement, and I had no plan.

I was a dreamer with an imaginative soul. I had colossal expectations, but the game plan was missing. I had no measurable goals. Would I achieve my dreams by magic? I created an image of myself without substance. It was a façade, a protective veneer. I desperately wanted others to see me as I wanted to be. There was a great internal struggle taking place. That inner turmoil continued throughout my adult life. I was struggling to find my real identity but it was only during the last three years, with the encouragement, support and Bonnie's belief in me, that I began to make progress.

You already know I am not a Ph.D. Even though I do not have an advanced degree, I do possess a modicum of intelligence and an abundance of common sense. While admittedly not religious, I have always had a strong belief in God. In fact, as long as I can recall, I have had daily conversations with my creator.

Where am I now, and how have I changed? As I approach my sixtieth birthday, I have learned to take daily reality checks on my life. I am focusing in the present moment. I accept my life has not been a bowl of cherries but rather a mixed bowl of assorted fruits, some ripe, some rotten.

I continue to ask myself a lot of questions. Most importantly, how can I create my future? Where am I going? If my trip was abruptly cancelled, what would be my contribution? What is my life's significance? What is **my** personal measuring stick of success? What is the barometer for **your** success? Life should be a plan, do, review, process. Regrettably, for most of us it is not. We take life for granted. Not a good idea! It can be snatched from us at any given moment, without reason, without explanation and without any advance notice.

As I began my search for the soul of my significance, I realized that many other people are struggling in search of significant lives of their own. They cannot seem to see the sun through the clouds. The following was on a greeting card sent to my friend Pete upon the death of his father. I find it to be true in life.

> **"Most of the battles in life are won**
> **By looking beyond the clouds to the sun**
> **And by having the patience to wait for the day**
> **When the sun comes out and the clouds go away."**

Almost everyone I talk with laments that they do not have time or money to do what makes them happy. Why not? What's their excuse? Do they expect success to one day arrive on their doorstep in a neatly wrapped UPS package? There is something alarming about this picture. In short, many people are leading very stressful, unhappy, and unproductive lives. Does this scenario sound familiar? The never ending search for the best within them is still stuck in the starting blocks. The twins of Purpose and Passion have not yet been born. Change scares them because they are glued to their old thought process of negativity and toxic behavior. Habit is the captain of their cruise through life. Navigating their lives by habit, they expect things to get better, yet they are unwilling to embrace the personal changes that are necessary to create the life of abundance they desire and deserve.

I WAS A CHARTER MEMBER OF THEIR CLUB!

In our lives there are rules for everything. Rules for business, rules at work, rules for parenting, rules for driving, rules for golf, relationships, divorce, dating and even our own self-imposed rules. How easily we follow someone else's rules. Oddly enough, when it comes to the rules for our lives, we have a difficult time defining them. When defined, we seem to have even more difficulty following them.

The scripts of our lives will undergo many rewrites and the cast of characters will be lengthy. While many of the social, technological, and economic changes will not be our fault, or our accomplishments, they will **always** be part of our lives. We seem to have a love/hate affair with life. When life is good, we feel good; when life is bad, we feel bad. How about when life is over? How will we feel then? We must acknowledge that while life is the biggest risk of all, it also brings us our greatest rewards.

PAUSE AND PONDER:

Where is my focus?

How do I manage the challenges in my life?

Can I manage alone? Who can help me?

We all expect health, wealth, and eternal happiness. Expecting something does not make it happen. Success does not happen by external combustion. It comes from an internal power source that propels us forward. It is a mixture of desire, energy, attitude, purpose, courage, risk, imagination and vision, sprinkled with enthusiasm, mixed with spirituality, and blended together as fuel for a belief system that is unstoppable.

Slowly and cautiously, I am tiptoeing out of my comfort zone. It has taken a long time. By nature and disposition, I am not a risk taker. Rocking the boat and making waves is uncomfortable. Avoiding conflict is paramount for me. I am a camper. When I find comfortable ground I prefer to stay there.

CHANGE IS A CONTINUAL PROCESS AND I AM CHANGING!

I am a work in progress. I have changed my thought processes, my attitude, my habits (not all but some), and my belief system. I have not changed the way I dress. I have changed what I read, what I listen to, and most of what I watch on television. I have strengthened my belief in God. I have changed the direction of my life, my career, and my purpose in life, I have found my passion.

I have discovered there is more to life than getting up in the a.m. and going to bed in the p.m. It is the time in between that really matters. It is what you do with your ideas, your energy and your dreams that makes the difference.

For most of my adult years, I was content to brush my teeth in the morning and again in the evening. Between those events, I worked, ate and went through the routine motions of daily existence. But I lived without purpose or passion. If you take time to discover what you do well (your family, friends, and colleagues will tell you), learn to do it better, pursue it with passion and strive for excellence, your life will have more meaning. Do not be good; be good at something. Discover what your *something* is. You do not have to be bulls-eye-perfect.

You will feel better about yourself if you stop wanting to be someone else. Direct your energies toward being the best you can be rather than focusing on what may never be. Happiness is always found within; take time to look for it. The color of the balloon does not make any difference. It is not what is on the outside that makes it rise; it is what is inside that makes it reach for the sky. Emerge from the cocoon called comfort zone. Brian Tracy, the noted sales trainer, has observed, "You can overcome fear and ignorance by desire and knowledge which will result in courage and confidence."

Life does not have a reverse gear. It is not a dress rehearsal for something else. You cannot write a sequel. Do not miss your only performance. Life is about growth. Growth is about change. Many of us only fly high enough to avoid the curb. *How high do you fly?* You will never discover new heights unless you leave the ground.

Do you really know and appreciate the face in the glass when you stare in the bathroom mirror? Does the mirror reflect your dreams, your motives, your desires and your goals? Of course not! The mirror cannot reflect what is in your heart, your mind, your attitude, or your spirituality. Our comfort zone is buried deep within us. Most of us are victims of a disease called *toxic negativity syndrome*. How many times have you heard, "you cannot do that," or "it is impossible," or "are you crazy, or "you are too old!" We are not taught to be possibility thinkers.

God never put any limitations on our lives. He created us all with an abundance of unlimited potential. Funny thing is, we are all given the same amount. I have never met anyone who had doctor, lawyer, CEO, or celebrity stamped on their birth certificate. No one is born with any guarantees. We are all born under the same sky, but we each seek our own horizons. To go anywhere, to do anything, calls for some timely decisions.

PAUSE AND PONDER:

Do YOU plan your life or does LIFE plan for you?

Are you in the driver's seat or just being transported like a passenger?

Do you have a need for speed and require instant gratification?

PERSONAL REFLECTIONS

PART THREE

DECISIONS

Decisions engage the gears of life. You can connect, get in motion and transverse a world of opportunity by making some wise, conscious choices that lead to positive actions.
Action produces results: massive action = massive results.

18

WHO ARE YOU?

**"Sometimes the best way to figure out
who you are is to go to a place where
you don't have to be anyone else."**

Unknown

Okay, so you're walking down the middle of a four-lane highway and suddenly there's a Mack truck bearing down on you. As it gets closer you hear the driver screaming at the top of his lungs,

"WHO ARE YOU?"

"WHO ARE YOU?"

"WHO ARE YOU?"

Just as the truck is about to shatter your bones, you wake up! Thank God it was only a dream! Yes indeed! But as we have seen in earlier chapters, the question demands an answer. **WHO ARE YOU?**

Have you ever met someone at a party or other networking opportunity who asked, "What do you do?" or "What keeps you busy?" I am sure you can provide a twenty-minute dissertation for an answer. Your response will either turn-on or turn-off the questioner, depending on your intention and their sincere interest. But, have you ever been asked, *"Who are you?"* Probably not! I'll bet you can convey a pretty good impression of who you are at job interviews. Why? Because you are able to rehearse your answers ahead of time. There **is** no rehearsal for life.

Suppose you were asked that same question but were prevented from stating anything that might be on your resume. You could not give your name, where you live, where you were born, what company you work for, what your job title is, what college you attended, what you majored in, what degree you received, whether or not you are married, have children, or what role you play in society.

The truth is that who you are is much bigger and far more important than what you **have** or what you **do**. So, **WHO ARE YOU**? It is an interesting question that you must face sooner or later. Take time to create a defining statement of yourself.

I am not asking you to do anything I have not done. True, I have had more time to think about it and I am asking you to write an immediate response. It was very difficult for me. It took a lot of soul searching and hard work. I am very different today. I realize that who I am has nothing to do with my career choices, my title, or how much money I earn.

You see, that was then and this is now! Those struggles, doubts and questions are in the past. I have wrestled with them and won. I have taken charge of my life. That is all I am really asking you to do: no more, no less. I take great pride in my new career path and it has given me great purpose for the rest of my life's journey.

This book is the result of my belief in myself and the unwaivering support of family and friends. I am slowly building a career as a professional speaker and author. Not bad for a sixty-year old. If I can do it **YOU** can do it! Just take your first step. That step starts with **believing** and **trusting** in yourself. *I challenge you to try it now.*

Take a notepad and see how much you can write in five minutes about yourself without referencing any of the things mentioned above. You will immediately see how difficult and challenging it is. You might not come up with anything for a minute or two. Even if you do, you will probably run out of things to say very quickly. In fact, you may just continue to stare at a blank piece of paper.

PAUSE AND PONDER:

Giving a percentage for each, determine how much of your identity is defined by the following:

	%
Job/Work	
Social Class	
Financial Situation	
Home	
Children	
Primary Relationship	
Church	
Education	
Gender	
Power	
Image	
Body	
Car	
Hobby	
Material Wealth	

Do not be surprised if your total adds up to nearly 100 percent. Society expects us to evaluate and define ourselves according to such a ledger.

That is how it was for me. I remember making choices with total disregard of the effect they were having on my life and for whom I was becoming as a result . I had lived a yacht and champagne lifestyle. I owned a luxury car, draped myself in designer clothes, traveled at will and surrounded myself with female companionship. My self-created image was **my** reality.

The **true** reality was that I was earning a beer and pretzels living and had become an expert at deficit spending and managing credit card debt. I had succumbed to society's prescription for success.

WARNING: Society's prescription is bad for your health.

Society, our families and our friends tend to define our success in terms of who we know, what we wear and our net worth. The deceased billionaire Malcolm Forbes said, "Wealth and worth are very rarely related." An intuitive but anonymous scholar stated it differently. He said, "The real measure of our wealth is our worth if we lost all our money."

We have worn the masks and played the roles so well that we have truly bought into the idea that our worth is defined by our jobs, our cars, our titles, the size of our homes and other symbols of status granted to us by society. Many of us believe we have no need to look beyond those symbols for the truth about who we are. Consequently, we really do not know who the real us is. **It's OK.** While there is nothing wrong about not knowing who we really are, isn't it more valuable when we make that discovery? Do you have the courage to be honest with yourself?

Remember that in Chapter Three I mentioned that according to Carl Jung we spend the first half of our life integrating our ego by gaining mastery over our life, creating wealth, power, and status in the community. He said we spend the second half breaking it down to gain mastery over ourselves. Frankly, that's OK. It is part of the process of life. It becomes a problem if we get stuck in the first phase and resist going into the second phase.

It is when we move into the second phase that we begin to define ourselves in terms of who we are inside. This definition separates us from wealth, power and what we do to earn a living. Remember, we are human *beings,* not human *doings.* It ceases to be a matter of what we **do**, it becomes a question of who we **are**. In other words, what is **our** authenticity? How do we show up in the world? I showed up with a tremendous need to impress other people. I dressed in designer clothes and became a master at name-dropping.

Most of us own objects of value for which we seek authentication of their worth. We get our homes appraised, our jewelry appraised, our artwork appraised, our cars appraised, in order to determine their true value. Perhaps, as human beings, we should seek an independent appraisal of our lives. That way we can determine our worth or value in the present moment and see if our worth increases or decreases in value as we continue the remaining journey of our lives.

When we define ourselves in terms of how we show up in life, we use terms like loving, generous, giving, caring, open, sexy, enthusiastic, energetic, cool, intelligent, optimistic, depressed, forgiving, macho, feminine and many, many more. In addition to some positive attributes, I showed up as angry, impatient and very critical of myself.

PAUSE AND PONDER:

Take a few moments and list for yourself some qualities that define who you are, or how you appear to the world.

Notice that whatever list you initially create, the seemingly important things such as wealth, power, image and status only showcase what is most unreal and unauthentic about you. They are simply things that are attached to you only so long as they stay attached. All of them are contingent qualities that can easily be taken away from you as some of you may have already found out. I did.

I mentioned earlier that in August 1995, I was hired to turn around a mismanaged and financially troubled company in Atlanta. Bonnie and I moved from the Washington, D.C. area, and I began my new challenge. Seven months later, I was stripped of my income, my self-esteem, and my sense of self-worth. I lost my job because a wealthy, self-serving individual unilaterally decided that it was no longer in his personal or business interest to continue business as usual. He had other plans, and they did not include his company or me. He would sell, and the chips would fall where they may. That was it! That was all!

His decision to sell the company left me unemployed. Fortunately, most of the other employees were able to continue working for the new owner. I respected his decision to sell, but I was shocked by the unprofessional manner in which I was informed. It is quite startling when you return from a business trip, find an attorney sitting behind your desk, and he tells you quite matter-of-factly that your services are no longer required. I know now that a job, in a way, is like life. It can be taken away from you at anytime without advance notice.

Now go back to that initial list of yours. Look at what attributes or qualities you really value. Think again about their real value. Think about what is *extrinsic* to your real self and derived only from your relationships with your environment. How transient they can be. How insecure you must be. How disillusioning they will be in the end. Now think of those things that are genuinely *intrinsic* to you. They are derived only from who you are on the inside. They define the real you. They are out of reach to anyone else. How rich you can be. How relaxed you must be. How satisfying they will be in the end.

So, could you be role-playing? Are you appearing to be what you are not and avoiding your true self? Are you skirting the real issues? You see, in order to be these things and play these roles, you wear many masks that, more often than not, conceal who you truly are even from yourself.

Now, make a decision to strip away the façade and come to terms with the intrinsic elements. Revise your list. Work at it. You will find that the attributes in your revised list, both good and bad, that define who you are, at this present time, is actually what is real and authentic about you. Of course, it is true only if you are telling the truth. It is very possible to be wearing a loving mask and not be loving at all, or one of serenity and be enduring a raging turmoil within.

Let me give you an example. Recent events have shown us that the President of the United States, whomever that might be at any time, is not his Office. That individual just happens to have the title and is attached to the office for a short period of time, four years or eight years. The press and media have shown us that the President is a person with strengths and weaknesses-- like us all. The choices he or she makes within himself, for himself, for his personal growth, have little to do with the job he happens to have, the title he holds, or whether or not he is in the public eye. The President, after all, is simply another human being.

He must live with himself, not his office. He must wrestle with his own values and integrity concurrently with the affairs of state. His greatest needs are more challenging than Secret Service protection. He must protect himself from himself. He must conquer the stress within. We may have a difficult time dealing with this reality precisely because it is hard for us to come out from behind our masks and be authentic ourselves. It is always so much easier to criticize human weakness than condone it.

But then, it is not only those icons in high office or with profiles larger than life who must pierce the cocoon. We each struggle with false appearance and make believe. When we begin to look at ourselves under the microscope to find our authentic selves, we often discover things we do not like and are not willing to accept. Carl Jung referred to this as our **shadow**. This is the part of us that may be controlling, manipulative, untrustworthy, and in some instances, criminal.

Jung showed that we tend to reject and deny our shadow side. We repress the feeling associated with it (guilt, anger, frustrations, etc.) and then project our shadow onto others. We then criticize them for the very things we subconsciously hate in ourselves so we can feel good about ourselves. Of course, all this happens without our conscious awareness.

This whole process is well described by Colin Tipping in his recent book *Radical Forgiveness*. (New Visions Press, 1997). Tipping says, "If you want to know what it is about yourself that you don't like and have repressed, just take note of what upsets you about other people. Absolutely, without exception, they are mirroring your own qualities back to you. This is to give you the opportunity to accept them and love them as yourself because they are YOU! You cannot be a whole person without accepting everything about yourself, both good and bad. When you forgive and accept the person who is upsetting you, you actually forgive and accept yourself. This is radical forgiveness and it is automatic."

It would be helpful for you to review the inventory you made earlier of all your qualities, both positive and negative. Be honest and add some others that are not so attractive. Look to see whom in your life is mirroring those for you. Stay away from the temptation to judge yourself. Just observe them. Remember there is nothing static or fixed about them. I said earlier you can be extremely loving in one moment and very unloving in another moment. The key is knowing the difference and allowing it to be okay either way. This ambivalence is the essence of being human.

PAUSE AND PONDER:

Whom do you model?

What qualitites do you admire in other people that you don't have?

Whom have you forgiven during the last 12 months?

PERSONAL REFLECTIONS

19

WHAT'S YOUR SCRIPT?

**"The difference between life
and the movies is that a
script has to make sense, and life doesn't."**

Joseph Mankiewicz

A life script contains a pattern of ideas and beliefs usually formed early in life. Those ideas and beliefs largely determine how we create the rest of our lives.

Life is not an accident, but parts of it may be accidental. It is very much a playing out of our unconscious beliefs and attitudes. Life does not care whether our beliefs are true or whether they are good or bad. It simply serves up what we want to be right about. In other words, we subconsciously create our life so that it is totally consistent with our script.

Let me illustrate. My script was similar to the daily

soap operas, *Days of Our Lives* and *As The World Turns.* The story line was always being written and rewritten in real time. Each episode was different. Different jobs, different cities, and different affairs of the heart. I was always looking for ratings or approval. I was never scripted for long term success but rather for short-term ratings. I never received a daytime Emmy.

In 1990, as I began my relationship with Bonnie, I discovered stability, support, security, nurturing, account- ability, dependability, and intimacy. Family and home life became my focus. **Trust, truth, teach, talk,** and **touch** became the pillars on which we have built the foundation of our marriage.

Up to that point, I was living out of control like a fugitive from life. I finally got tired from running and turned myself in. Now I am scripting a more enlightened and enriched life.

Here are some ideas, both negative and positive, that commonly form lifescripts for people—people just like you and me.

Life is a struggle
Life is easy
I'll never be good enough
I'm OK

I don't deserve
I deserve
Success means those I love leave
Success is good
Money corrupts people
Money can do good
We were born to be…..
Life is opportunity
I'm just like my parents
I'll never be like my parents
There is never enough
Life is abundant
All men hurt me, leave me
I am safe with
The world is an unsafe place
I will always be taken care of

These ideas, and we usually have a myriad of them, are tucked away in our subconscious mind and act like internal gyroscopes to keep our lives synchronized with those beliefs.

If your script is that the world is an unsafe place, that when people become successful they leave, that you live in a world of scarcity, you do not deserve to have

nice things, and that all wealthy people are basically cor-
rupt, guess what kind of life you have created? You can
place a winning bet that your life will be one which
creates a lot of drama around issues of safety, crime and
accidents; people will leave you when they become successful; you will always be poor no matter how hard you
try to make money; in fact, if you ever make money,
someone will rob you. If you want to know what your
script is, just **scrutinize your life**.

At age fifty-six, I rewound the video of my life and
began to realize I had created a whole lot of struggle,
failure, abandonment and rejection. Somewhere along
the way, I made a subconscious decision that life was
about living on the edge. I believed the only way to
please people, such as my family, friends, and first wife,
was to appear successful. In otherwords, *fake it 'til you
make it.* That belief system sent me messages that I was
never going to be successful because I was not good
enough, and my efforts would always be rejected--a
double, double whammy. It was, no doubt, much more
complicated than that.

Now it does not really matter. Today, my belief
system tells me I can do anything, and if it is to be, it is
simply up to me.

Let's look at the bright side. Whatever script you

follow, you produced it. It may be just a load of garbage, nothing more, nothing less. But none of the ideas that form your script may have any basis in reality. They are not concrete or cast in stone. They are simply a multitude of intangible ideas that some child made up. That little child was you. Vulnerable and malleable as you were then, you inculcated the ideas and adopted the role that played them out.

Those subconscious habits are very resistant to change. They cause inner turmoil and frequently cause others confusion and concern.

If you don't like the script you wrote, rewrite it!

For example, as I rewrote my life's script, I became an anomaly to my family and friends. They could accept, respect and support my decision, or they could shrug their shoulders in disbelief. It was their choice. I had made mine. With a long sigh of relief, I took a stand for my life. I spent a lot of "quiet" time questioning my worth as a provider, a husband, a father and as a man. It was an agonizing, nervous, nail-biting time in my life.

While I was employed, it was so much easier for others to accept me as a normal, productive member of society. As a corporate executive, I felt respected because of my title, my position and my salary. My perception was that losing my job and not being the *bread-*

winner stripped me of their respect.

Had I chosen to restore the scripted status quo, accept a position, a title and a predictable daily routine, that choice would have been comfortable for my family and friends, but not for my wife and not for me.

I set myself free from the expectations of others and began to follow expectations I had established for myself. While this decision was liberating--it caused eyebrows to raise. Frankly, it did not matter to me anymore. I had stepped across the threshold from security to uncertainty. I had made my choice to become a speaker and an author. I felt in my heart that I was on the right path, and in the end, that is all that matters.

My decision to become a speaker/author was relatively easy. I loved speaking, and writing a book would be a challenge. My wife was my strongest supporter both emotionally and financially. My awareness of relying solely on Bonnie's financial resources for a period of time placed me in a very dependent frame of mind. Recognizing I was not the breadwinner took its emotional toll and I felt extremely inadequate. Realizing what people were thinking, I was in a world of hurt. All my life I had been a giver, not a taker, by giving to everybody--but not to myself. I was always a man of **presents,** and now I was becoming a man of **presence**. Shedding the fabric of guilt, I have given *myself* a gift--significance. I was in a place in my life where I needed help. I had to confront the facts, deal with them and accept help as offered.

It did not only effect me. Initially, it was also a very difficult time for my wife. While unwavering in her love for me and totally in support of my decision, it caused some momentary uneasiness in her life. We have had many discussions about our "role reversal." Through mutual respect, unquestionable faith and trust in each other, and a love that grows stronger each day, my decision is no longer an issue. In fact, **my** decision became **our** decision. Bonnie and I have been blended in God's mixer, and we are forever joined at the soul.

If you are married, involve your spouse from the start. If you are not married, involve your family, friends or other significant people in your life. Remember, it is always about being vulnerable and sharing your fears and dreams. When you show your vulnerability, you will be amazed at how quickly you will receive the support you need.

Realize, a conscious decision alone will not change your script. You have to change it at the subconscious level. How do you accomplish that feat?

The first step is to determine what your life script is. Again, you can do this by taking a look at what has shown up in your life, both good and bad. Also, try to recall what you learned about life as a child. What did you learn about life, prosperity, success, the kind of work or career you should have, and so on? For example, can you imagine any of the Kennedy children being scripted by their parents to be dirt farmers or starving artists? Not even for one minute. No, their scripts enabled their subconscious minds to foresee themselves as Senators and Presidents. What were you predetermined to be? If you do not like the video of your life thus far, you now have the opportunity to change it.

I did! You can too.

Make a list of the ideas and beliefs you think might be central to your script. Then craft a statement that you want your subconscious mind to accept in place of any limiting belief. This is known as an affirmation.

For example:

Existing limiting belief: "I don't want money because those who have money are exploitive, pompous and often nasty people."

Replacement Affirmation: "People do good in the world with their money. I will do good with all the money I'm attracting to myself."

Existing limiting belief: "No matter what I do, it is never enough. I will never succeed."

Replacement Affirmation: "I am so talented and capable. Everyone appreciates and loves my work."

Existing limiting belief: "I don't want success because people become unhappy or leave when success occurs." (This is the fear of success)

Replacement Affirmation: "I can have success in my life and be happy at the same time."

Existing limiting belief: "I always have do to things for myself."

Replacement Affirmation: "I can ask for help and people will help me whenever I need support."

Existing limiting belief: "Life is always a struggle. Nothing comes easy to me."

Replacement Affirmation: "Life can be easy if I trust in life and abundance will follow."

Work on your own limiting beliefs and create affirmations that really feel good to you. Visualize them and place copies of them wherever you might see them— on your bathroom mirror, in your car, in your office and in your billfold. Put them everywhere. I talk to myself everyday, in the shower, the car, while walking and even in the bathroom. I continually affirm what I expect my life to be by identifying it in the present tense. I will continue to do so until each affirmation becomes a reality.

Notice that the above affirmations are written in the present tense. The subconscious does not understand **future**. Always write as if what you want is happening in the present moment. Faithfully stating your affirmations on a regular basis is the quickest and most effective way to make changes in your subconscious mind.

PAUSE AND PONDER:

Select one of your new affirmations and then repeat it audibly as often as you can until it travels the 14 inches from your head to your heart. You will see the life transformation it creates.

What unrehearsed scripts are keeping you from pursuing your goals and dreams?

Be prepared for resistance from family, friends, co-workers and others, to the changes you are making. When you change your script, you become a different person. Things start happening to you that many of your family, friends and co-workers may not understand.

PERSONAL REFLECTIONS

20

WHAT'S YOUR PASSION?

**"There is no greatness
without passion to be great,
whether it's the aspiration of an athlete
or an artist, a scientist, a parent,
or a businessperson."**

Anthony Robbins

You will recall in Chapter 9, I related how Bonnie sprang a surprise question on me. She chose her moment carefully so that I would not have time to reflect about it. I had to respond immediately. Her question was, "What makes you most happy?" In an instant, I replied, "Public speaking. I love talking to audiences and telling stories." I had spent several years in Toastmasters, an international organization that supports people who wish to improve their speaking skills. I quickly learned I did not have a fear of public speaking.

This was probably the most important healing moment in my whole story. It meant that I had found my passion. What's more, I had given voice to it. I had claimed it. I took ownership of it. I had affirmed my passion.

In spite of self-doubt, and a lot of mind talk that tried to convince me that I could not be a successful speaker, did not have the skills, was too old, did not have the knowledge, was not humorous enough and others, I triumphed. At that moment I began to transform my life. I aligned with my inner compass. I acknowledged that authentic part of me which I knew would make my heart sing. It was my *Hallmark* moment.

When I answered Bonnie's question so spontaneously and left no room for reason or analysis, I did so without regard to how much money I might be able to earn, how I would find audiences that would listen to me and who would hire me. **It was my moment of truth.** There were no conditions or expectations.

PAUSE AND PONDER:

Suppose someone were to ask you the same question, right now. How would you answer? What is it

that makes your heart sing? What would make you leap out of bed in the morning and just do it?

Are you doing something right now that does not really fit who you are? Are you employed in a job because it pays well and you get benefits that you are afraid to lose? Are you a wage slave?

Did you go into a career because you were scripted to do that type of work? Are you a square peg in a round hole as I was for thirty years?

If you dislike what you are doing to earn a living-- **REGROUP!** It is not a matter of life and death but there is something sad about doing work that you dislike just for money. How many government employees or corporate junkies would jump that nine-to-five ship of monotonous routine and office politics if the paycheck were not guaranteed? How many street-corner lawyers would continue to practice law if the money was lousy and the status of the job was lowered? The same would be true for many overworked and stressed-out physicians working in the profit-driven, bottom-line, health management system we refer to as health care.

Rapid change is an integral part of our lives. The

belief that you will have the same job or follow the same career for your entire life is an obsolete idea. For me, I felt trapped within the walls of Corporate America. I did not see any alternative. It goes back to the issue of change. While it was not the panacea, guess what? I chose to stay in my comfort zone. Sound familiar?

In reality, surveys have shown that the typical person today will have five different types of employment. It means doing one thing today and something else tomorrow. Sooner or later, you are likely to change your job or career. So, if you are not passionate about what you do, why not consider something else that might ignite your internal engine?

That sounds simple. I know many of you will say, "Yea, right. It's not that easy. How about the mortgage payments? What about the car payments, college for the kids, and other financial obligations?"

Look, life is a trade-off. It is all about making choices. It is about priorities. If your job title, fancy cars, big house and lots of material possessions are more important than pursuing your passion, so be it. The choice is yours. I am not suggesting that you give up your current income. We all have to put food on the table and pay our bills. Following your passion does not necessarily mean choosing between your passion and putting food on the table. It may get you beyond the bottleneck you face, whatever that is, or maybe it simply means returning to school and studying for a new and more creative career. It may trigger something new and big. It may allow a better opportunity to come to you. Perhaps, it will lead to a more fulfilling lifestyle. Who is to say? All you can do is just trust the process.

PAUSE AND PONDER:

Going for your passion may be a risk. Ask yourself, is it a risk worth taking? What do you really have to lose? What might be your reward?

If you are on a certain career path that you are not passionate about but cannot cut the cord right now, that is OK. Continue, and at least make it a conscious choice.

Most of us do not make these choices consciously. We tend to buy into the thinking of other people and what they believe is best for us. We allow family and friends and professional persuaders, to manipulate us without realizing it. We buy into the idea that success is having more things, looking more important, having more money, buying a bigger house, a nice car and so on.

That insures we keep working to purchase more of the useless things we deem necessary to show our success to the outer world. We are the grist mill, and who really cares if we enjoy our job or not as long as we keep the wheels of commerce turning?

Whatever you choose, you must understand the trade-off. The price of anything you choose in your life is that which you gave up in order to have what you have chosen. Once you make the choice, the choice controls the chooser...**YOU.**

PAUSE AND PONDER:

What have you chosen to give up to have your present lifestyle? Freedom? Mobility? Creativity? Integrity? Satisfaction? Quality time with your spouse, children, family and friends? Peace of mind?

Often it is not until we stop, look, listen and understand how we have structured our lives that we realize how we have trapped ourselves. We begin to understand the treadmill we are on. We then convince ourselves that we are trapped and cannot walk away from it all. Yes, we can! We built the prison and we can tear it down and free ourselves, anytime we desire. **Desire** is the keyword.

Here is what I have observed to be true. When I make conscious choices in the direction of living in alignment with my passion and purpose and what is congruent with who I truly am, the universe supports me. When I declared to Bonnie that I wanted to become a speaker, I affirmed it. I did not know how I would achieve my goal, how long it would take, what resources would be necessary, and what opportunities would present themselves. I just made a conscious decision to do it.

Many of you will say, "Suppose I don't know what I'm passionate about?" "What if I have no idea what I would really like to do with the rest of my life?" That's OK. A lot of people are in that position. Some are so separated from their feelings that they have a difficult time registering anything emotional. For them, the solution is to work on getting in touch with their feelings so they will understand how they *feel* in relation to what they *do*. For others, it may simply be they have not yet discovered their passion and are still in the *search* mode. If this is true for you, just be patient and keep searching. Ultimately, it will become evident as it did for me. Maybe you had acknowledged until reading this book that you were not getting the satisfaction you deserve from your career or your lifestyle. If so, self-discovery is taking place.

Wherever you are in this process, if your career or lifestyle is not satisfying or fulfilling, the important thing is to make a commitment to yourself to begin the search. Find whatever will be meaningful and rewarding in your life. Once you have made that discovery, trust that the universe will respond and abundance will come. Where there is doubt, there can be no trust. Where there is trust, there can be no doubt.

21

WHAT DO YOU VALUE?

**"The major value in life is not what you get.
It's what you become."**

Jim Rohn

Values give us our moral compass. Our western value system is founded upon certain clear principles. Among these are fairness, honesty, truth, integrity, freedom, respect for others, equality and justice. Political values include freedom of speech, equal justice before the law and democratic rights. Qualities like compassion, humility, tolerance and forgiveness also connect to our value system.

You are most authentic and most alive when you talk about what you value--that which has real meaning for you. These are core values, and they form the essence of your character. As such, they provide clues as to who you really are and what you stand for.

What you value may also include the ordinary and mundane. The often unnoticed things in life like a beautiful sunset, a barefoot walk on wet grass, the twinkle in an old man's eye, a baby crying, blooming flowers and trees, and stimulating conversation are often ignored.

Any good self-evaluation requires taking inventory of your values. Bonnie and I recently did the following exercise together.

EXERCISE:
This activity is designed to help you and someone you care about (spouse, significant other, or close friend) identify what you each value most. For this exercise to be effective, you must participate individually.

With two sets of index cards write each of the following values, **one per card:** trust, family, self-esteem, money, compassion, joy, friends, health, spirituality, intimacy, respect, integrity and success. (In otherwords, put each value on its own card and one set for each of you).

Now for the challenging part.

Put the cards in order of their value to you, the most important having the highest priority. Compare with each other.

Were you surprised at the results? Are you spending your time on what you value the most?

Values reflect the importance you attach to issues of principle. At the deepest level, they are issues over which you might give your life rather than compromise. At the level of everyday life and the challenges it presents, they represent those issues that you are most likely to get into arguments over, or even lose your job over. They also underpin the very structure of your lives and give meaning to what you do.

When we live in harmony with our values, we tend to be happy and content. Conversely, when we live our lives contrary to our basic values, we begin to experience dissatisfaction, depression and disillusionment.

Another way to find out what your core values are, is to ask yourself the following questions.

1. What do you get upset about, passionate about, or preoccupied about?
2. What are you willing to take a stand for?
3. What kinds of causes do you support, for the sake of the cause itself, not for **what's in it for you?**
4. What moral values always get your attention in a newspaper or magazine?
5. What kinds of values would you risk your career, your livelihood, or your life for?

6. If you had to choose three qualities to have in your life, what would be at the top of the list?

Each of us has our own value system. What is important to me may not be important to you. The critical point is that each of us live our lives congruent with what we value.

PAUSE AND PONDER:

How easily do you compromise your values for a short--term advantage? Do you take a strong stand on issues, or do you believe flexibility to be more important than remaining rigid? Are you for sale? (Can you be bought?) At what cost? Where do you draw the line?

Now let us get back to the principles or values in your life. Big picture issues are interesting and important, but at the end of the day, it is how values translate into your daily life that is really important. How are you impacted each day psychologically, emotionally and spiritually by society's prevailing value system? How real is your so-called freedom?

Is a system driven by greed and selfishness as noble

as we would like to believe? Is our preoccupation with money costing us our soul and our significance? Is **competition** more valuable than **cooperation** and **community**? Do we become so attached to our *toys* that we have forgotten what is meaningful and fulfilling in life? Is our need for security simply an illusion we create? Is there any security at all in material things? How much freedom do we really enjoy if we are married to a job we dislike, have a large 30-year mortgage, a car payment, kids in school, insurmountable credit card debt and other social and financial obligations hanging from our necks?

I know there are no pat answers to these questions. However, that does not mean that we can ignore them. The answers provide a key to making better sense of our lives and arriving at better choices.

Today, millions of people live their lives out of alignment with their values. Disliking their work, feeling trapped by their circumstances, victimized, lonely and unfulfilled, they are searching for something better.

PAUSE AND PONDER:

You got lucky. You won the Lottery!
Five Million Dollars!
What would you change about your life?

If this happened to you it is a safe bet to say your value system would change immediately. What you believed to be important would suddenly seem totally irrelevant. You might even stop working to spend more time with your children, family and friends. The large house you always dreamed about becomes less important as well as the expensive roadster you had to have.

The question to ask yourself is, Why do I have to wait for a **happening,** good or bad, to wake me up? Why can't I see what's important and meaningful now, in the present moment? Why am I not willing to give up the life everyone expects of me rather than doing what I should really expect from myself?

I am not suggesting we should be irresponsible. There are certain things we are committed to doing and have to continue. We do, however, often impose far more burdens upon ourselves than necessary.

We are more flexible than we imagine ourselves to

be. We live unshackled within the walls of a prison of our own construction and sometimes, even when the cell door is left open, we still refuse to leave. Why? Our self-imposed prison is too comfortable and, in some cases, not comfortable at all. Perhaps it is the fear of the unknown that stops us from making changes in an effort to *enjoy* our lives more. Who knows what might happen if we set ourselves free from our self--imposed comfort zone.

Examine what is important to you and determine what is not. Get rid of all that is unimportant in your life. Focus your time and energies on what will have meaning in your life, and gradually get rid of the other *stuff*.

It may seem somewhat ridiculous, but begin by cleaning out all your closets, cupboards, drawers, office, garage and basement. I challenge you to throw out all but the most essential items. You see, the garbage that you have cluttering up your house is a great metaphor for the garbage you have allowed to clutter up you life. Get rid of it! **Simplify your life.** The less *clutter* in your life, the better you will feel. Strengthen the things in your life that make you happy.

PERSONAL REFLECTIONS

22

LIVING THE LIFE YOU LOVE

**"Trust yourself. Create the kind of self
you will be happy to live with all your life.
Make the most of yourself by fanning
the tiny, inner sparks of possibility into
flames of achievement."**

Foster C. McClellan

What are you doing with the business of your life? You have only one and there is no dress rehearsal. Life is an exciting journey. Make sure you take a lot of pictures and enjoy the trip. Your life is like raw material. You can sculpt your existence into something beautiful or you can chisel it into something ugly. It is in your hands.

You have read and heard about re-engineering the corporation. What about re-engineering your life? Now may be the best time to do an audit of your lifestyle.

Ask yourself three questions:

Do I **want** the lifestyle I have?
Do I **have** the lifestyle I deserve?
Do I **deserve** the lifestyle I want?

Lifestyle is a serious business, and it is not about working nine-to-five. It is not about profit and loss, sales calls, quotas, forecasts and balance sheets. It is about **YOU**. Lifestyle is about living **your** life, **your** way. It is more about a **life** style rather than a **style** of life.

John Homer Miller said, "Living is really determined not so much by what happens to you as by the way your mind looks at what happens to you. Circumstances, family, friends and situations do color life, but **YOU** have been given the mind to chose what the color will be."

Do not suffer from an LSD mentality. I am not talking about the choice psychodelic drug of the fifties and sixties. I am talking about *Limiting Self Decisions* or *Limiting Self Doubts*. Break through the mental ceiling that is holding you back from achieving the lifestyle you deserve.

What follows is my formula for a balanced lifestyle.

RISK + CHANGE X ATTITUDE = LIFESTYLE
TIME

Risk is your personal travel agent that will chart the journey of your life. Have the courage to risk. It is essential. The energy of risk-taking will attract others to help you achieve your goal. Nothing is going to happen that you cannot handle and you already have all of the skills you will need. Life moves forward with risk and so will you. People who fail in life see the risk in every opportunity while those who succeed always see opportunity in every risk. What do you see?

You cannot go through life without risk. It is impossible.

"When you **laugh,** you **risk** appearing the fool.
When you **love,** you **risk** not being loved in return.
To **expose** your true feelings is to **risk** exposing yourself.
When you **reach out** for another, you **risk** involvement.
When you **try,** you **risk** failure."

Anonymous Chicago Schoolteacher

Risk is your constant companion. You take it everywhere you go. You cannot leave home without it. It is often calculated and often spontaneous. Let me give you an example:

It was Tuesday, August 19, 1985. I had just exited the Fulton County Courthouse in Atlanta, Georgia after my divorce hearing.

I drove my 1983 Audi station wagon to Atlanta's Hartsfield International Airport and parked it in a predetermined spot. I had sold the car to my attorney's friend, and he was to pick it up later that evening.

Around 7:00p.m, I boarded a Delta flight to Germany where I would make my home for the next three and a half years.

I had accepted a job with an American systems integration company in Wiesbaden, West Germany. It was a difficult decision. I was both emotionally and financially drained. I saw the move as a way of regaining my confidence and meeting my court determined financial obligations. I knew it was a good opportunity for me, but it was a calculated risk.

I was moving to a foreign country. I did not speak the language, I did not know anyone and would have to find a place to live. To make matters worse, I was leaving my family, friends and two young children behind. Considering the difficult time I had in my first marriage, you may be questioning my judgement in leaving my children in the total care of their mother. I was not concerned. I trusted her parenting skills.

Living in a foreign country, working for an American company afforded me a tax-free status. Psychologically, I knew this would ease my pain and help restore my financial stability.

I weighed the risk of being away from my children against the opportunity of rebuilding my self-esteem, getting back on my feet financially, and having my children visit me in Europe. I concluded the opportunity was worth the risk. I was right.

Each time my children came to visit afforded us the opportunity to be together and explore different parts of Europe. We tobogganed in the mountains of Switzerland, revisited history in Rome, London and other European cities. We attended the Wimbledon Tennis Championships. To this day, we continue to talk about our wonderful once in a lifetime experiences.

The second ingredient in the formula is CHANGE.

Change is really the essence of life. It is the foundation upon which you can build your personal growth. In order to continue living and to keep on growing, you must keep on changing on the inside and remake yourself everyday. If you want to understand change you just have to look in the mirror. Believe it or not, you are changing each and every day. The faster your life changes, the more it stretches your ability and willingness to adapt.

Hundreds of years ago, change took place so slowly that we hardly noticed. Today it happens almost every time you blink your eye. If you have a natural tendency to adapt quickly to change you will have a much easier time than those who are slow to adjust. Position yourself to be on the crest of change and not behind the wave.

We have a love/hate relationship with change. Too much change makes us uneasy. All of us would like things to remain the same but at the same time get better. But it does not work in that way. We can always have change without improvement, but we can rarely have improvement without change. Look for the opportunities of tomorrow in the changes of today.

Most of us are live in a hurry-and-worry world. We get up, get dressed, get in the car, get in the traffic, go to work, go home, go to bed and then do the same thing all over again the next day. Why? It's easy. It's called habit. We do not seem to understand that **habit** is the great stabilizer of human society, but it is **change** that propels society forward.

In April 1996, the company I was hired to turn-around was sold. I had no job, no money, no future. I was fifty-six years old, and everyone told me I should retire. I was not ready to expire or retire. After sending out several hundred resumes and receiving several polite letters of rejection, I was very discouraged.

I began to read and listen to motivational books and tapes. I read inspirational books. I attended success seminars. Still, nothing changed. I began to realize that books and tapes cannot change anything, no more than a recipe can bake a cake. In order for personal change to take place, I had to change.

I made a decision to change the direction of my life. I decided to become a professional speaker and author. My decision led to action and this book is the result. For fifty-six years, I did not think anybody listened to me. It now gives me great satisfaction as I speak before corporate audiences.

All change must begin from within. We easily change jobs, spouses, relationships, homes, cars and shoe. We rarely think about changing ourselves. Change can be difficult; it can also be rewarding. Our own personal change and growth is the most difficult task of all. If you change the inner aspects of your mind, you will change the outer aspects of your life. The profit will all be yours.

The common denominator in the formula is **TIME**.

Time has taught me alot over the last 40 years. Each year it seems to take less time to fly to Europe and longer to drive to work. If it were not for the last minute, nothing would get done. An investment in time usually pays the best interest. I have also learned that ordinary people tend to spend time but successful people think of using it.

Margaret B. Johnson said, "Time is like having fixed income. As with any fixed income, the real problem facing most of us is how to live successfully within our daily allotment."

To understand the value of one month, ask the mother who has given birth to a premature baby. To realize the value of one minute, ask the person who has just missed the bus, plane or train. To comprehend the value of one millisecond, just ask the athlete who won the Silver Medal at the Olympics.

Time waits for no one. You cannot slow it down and you cannot recycle it. Once you spend it, you can never get a refund. There is no return policy. You cannot politic with time.

Have you ever heard people say, *I'm just killing time?* Have you ever asked yourself why they are killing the time they are so desperately trying to save? The great dividing line between success and failure can be expressed in five words--"**I do not have time.**"

But to think of it, that is sheer folly. You always have the time for one thing or the other. The sun always rises on the just and the unjust, and the circle of life goes on. You **can** choose how to spend all your moments and all your days.

We have talked about **RISK** and **CHANGE** over **TIME.** How do we tie them all together? The answer is by maintaining a positive mental **ATTITUDE**.

Attitude is one of the most important words in our language. It is really the way you approach your life. It is the outward expression of your innermost thoughts and feelings. It tells others a lot about who you really are.

Your attitude is really determined by your expectations of life. Expectations come from beliefs. Your expectations about work, family, friends, relationships and people are generated by what you believe to be true in that specific area. Your beliefs will determine the quality of your personality and your performance.

W. Clement Stone said, "There is really very little

difference in people. But that **little** difference can make a **big** difference. The **little** difference is **ATTITUDE**. The **big** difference is whether it is **positive** or **negative**." Even if in the long run the pessimist may be right, the optimist will have a much better time on the trip.

Have you ever heard of the **FAILURE FACTOR** in life? Most people seem to have it. There are really only two ways to look at virtually anything. One is positive and the other is negative. It is like the ying and yang of the universe. You cannot develop eye strain from looking at the brighter side of life.

You can improve your attitude by:

1. Building solid relationships with positive and successful people.

2. Feeling good about your job and your workplace.

3. Preparing for the future.

4. Most importantly, **FEELING GOOD ABOUT YOURSELF**.

As   Robert Shuller has preached for years, you have to teach yourself how to focus on **POSSIBIL-ITY THINKING**. Look at **"IMPOSSIBLE** as **"I'M POSSIBLE."** Focus your energies on what you can control not on what you cannot control. Positive and creative thinking is the fuel of our mental lives. Ideas are born, they develop, reach maturity and die. Since your mind is your own private stage, you can give any new idea a private audition for a few days.

You can build positive mental strength the same way you build physical strength--by repetition. Working with weights builds physical strength. Manipulating positive thoughts builds mental strength. Unlike physical exercise, you will not wake up sore the next morning from a hard workout of mental exercise.

Your mind is really the garage where you park your ideas and your attitude. Focus on the opportunities of tomorrow and not on the problems of today. If you park good ideas and a positive attitude at night, you will wake up with good ideas and leave for life with a positive attitude in the morning. Your positive attitude leads to positive activity, which leads to positive results, which leads to a meaningful lifestyle.

You see, making a living and making a life that is worth living are not the same thing.

PAUSE AND PONDER:

What are you prepared to *risk* and *change* to create a more meaningful lifestyle?

PART FOUR
ACTIONS

"If I am not for myself,
who will be for me?
If I am not for others, what am I?
And if not now, when?"

Rabbi Hillel

23

IF NOT NOW, WHEN?

"Sometime in your life you will go on a journey. It will be the longest journey you have ever taken. It is the journey to find yourself."

Katherine Sharp

L̲et's journal! Why, you ask?

On September 17, 1996, my wife gave me a leather bound writing journal. It had my name engraved on its cover. The inscription on the first page read, *"As you capture on these pages the thoughts, experiences, observations and feelings of who you are, remember always that I am forever believing in you."*

My first entry on September 18, 1996 read, "…received this journal from my loving soulmate. Hopefully it will inspire me to write a book entitled, *Where's Your Gold Watch?* On October 26, 1996, I wrote, "...my goal is to have my book finished prior to Liz's wedding." Liz, my wife's daughter from a prior marriage, tied the knot in August of 1997. The book was still a work in progress. As you know, that book **is** finished and it is entitled, *Kiss Yourself Hello.*

Well, as I have said throughout the book, change happens at a rapid pace. For almost two years the book's original title was, *Where's Your Gold Watch?* I had created what I believed to be a great title and had pride of ownership. I had my business cards, promotional material and bookmarks printed with that title. It was my creation. There was no way I was going to change it. Until my literary agent, my graphic artist and several book reviewers convinced me otherwise. Their concern that *Where's Your Gold Watch?* might be misinterpreted as a book about jewelry (of all things) forced me to put my ego aside! As I stated earlier in the book, you can accept change by consent or coercion. I chose to accept the name change in the title by consent.

For me, daily journal writing was then and continues to be, a difficult feat. Even today I find myself allowing days and sometimes weeks to pass without making a journal entry. Not a good idea. I usually write *jog your memory* notes and then make full journal entries at a later time.

Over the last two years or so, I have kept a journal of significant events that have had an impact or influenced my life in some way. Recording my thoughts in a journal gives me a chance to go back and revisit events that were important to me. It also allows me to identify roadblocks. At the beginning of each year, I write my goals for the coming year and review my goals for the year past. It brings back vivid memories that I will cherish for a lifetime and that will be passed on to my children.

PAUSE AND PONDER:

Do you keep a daily journal? If you do, that's great! If not, why not?
Don't think it! Ink it!

It has been a long time since my stroll in the neighborhood and we have come a long way together. I hope the trip was meaningful and rewarding for you. For me, it has been both a difficult and enlightening journey of self-discovery.

I have found answers-- not all, but many. I am continually discovering **who I am.** I trust this book has helped you to discover **who you are.**

I have taken a long hard look in the mirror of my life. It has been revealing and at times painful. At first glance, I was not happy and had frequently been hard on myself.

Now, I am on the offensive of life. I am no longer waiting around for happy endings. I am creating my own endings and beginnings. I have uncovered my purpose and my passion. My sails are full and I am charting a course towards my own significance and legacy.

I am lovin' myself now. I am evolving into the person I want to be. It has not been an overnight process. I could not microwave myself; it is like slow cooking a roast. Over time, you get it the way you like it. I am slowly approaching the finish line.

I am a recovering, rehabilitated corporate junkie. The treatment was a rousing success. I know where I am going. I have given up the rigidity of my thought processes and pulled in my safety net. My life is now in overdrive.

By rescripting my life for success and significance, I am re-editing the video of my life. A new one is in process. Freed from the expectations of others, I am following the expectations and goals I set for myself.

The life I am living now is definitely the life **I have** chosen. It's not **where** you are in life that's important. It's not **what** you are in life that's important. What's important is **who** you are.

Throughout this journey, I have been honest with you. You must now be honest with yourself. Be deliberate in your choices but most of all be patient. It has taken me nearly 37 years to discover the **real** me. My wife and I are now pursuing the lifestyle we want and deserve.

Let's review the formula for the lifestyle **YOU** deserve.

$$\frac{\textbf{RISK + CHANGE}}{\textbf{TIME}} \quad \textbf{X} \quad \textbf{ATTITUDE = LIFESTYLE}$$

RISK is where your opportunities lie.

CHANGE is where your personal growth occurs.

TIME will become the currency of the 21st Century. Don't spend it; use it.

A **POSITIVE ATTITUDE** will not cause eyestrain.

As you finish this book, I would like to leave you with the following thoughts:

- **Accept Yourself:** You are one of a kind. Get to know yourself better. Shake hands with yourself more often. Discover the **you** in **you**rself. Do not get in your own way. Take the **if** out of **Life!**
- **Create Balance in Your Life:** Life is like a great puzzle. When you put all the pieces together, it creates a magnificent picture.
- **Share Your Abundance With Others:** Living is about giving. Whatever measure you use to give—large or small—will be used to measure what is given to you. The more you give to life, the more you will receive from life. Life is a wonderful treasure chest filled with precious moments. Share its wealth.
- **Cultivate A Forgiving Heart:** Flush out the acid of anger, and you will eliminate the burden of bitterness.
- **Ignite Your Internal Engine:** No excuses, just choices. Success does not happen by external combustion. You have to ignite your own fire.
- **Strive for Excellence:** Find out what you do well, and learn to do it better. You do not have to be bulls eye perfect. Only God is perfect.

- **Remember Your Past--Trust Your Future:** Your ability to relax in life is directly proportionate to your ability to trust in life.

Well, we have come to the end of **our** journey together. It is now time to begin **your** journey. Travel with energy and enthusiasm. Take lots of pictures. Create new friendships along the way. Acknowledge abundance in your life. Plan a great trip. Enjoy the **life**style you deserve. Because…

IT'S TIME TO *LISTEN,* TIME TO *LEARN,* TIME TO *LIVE…* **YOUR** LIFE… **YOUR** WAY!

HAVE A SUCCESSFUL JOURNEY

EPILOGUE

It has been a long time since my stroll in the neighborhood. To this day, I do not fully understand what happened to me in that moment. I am grateful that it did. It started me out on a fabulous journey of self-discovery.

How has it been for you? Meaningful and rewarding, I hope. Maybe it will be the start of you re-evaluating your life and moving in the direction of greater happiness and fulfillment.

For me, the process continues. I have found many answers, but not all. I know there is a lot more to learn about myself and life. I am discovering who I am in every moment, and I know this process will continue until I draw my last breath.

I have taken a long hard look in the mirror of my life. It has been revealing and at times painful. I do not regret one minute of it.

In the beginning, I was very unhappy with what I saw and extremely hard on myself. Now, I have compassion for Phil Parker and realize that I was doing the best I could at the time.

I am now on the offensive of life. I am no longer waiting around for happy endings or beginnings. I have discovered my purpose and passion, and I am pursuing them with an attitude of trust and confidence. I will not be persuaded to deviate from them, no matter what happens. Nothing is more important. Never again will I live out of insecurity, fear, obligation and convention. My sails are full, and I am charting a course toward my own legacy. I cherish the journey ...

I cherish the journey and know now that it took everything that happened and every second of those thirty-seven years to bring me to this point and I am grateful for it.

Now, I can honestly say that I am loving myself and creating the person I want to be. I accept myself totally the way I am – strengths, weaknesses and all.

I began this book believing I was writing it for the people who would read it to help them avoid the mistakes I had made. I now realize that I was writing it only for myself in order to understand that my experience were not mistakes at all, but part of my life's journey.

So, if you have traveled with me and learned something about yourself, that is a bonus.

I hope this book serves you well. Thank you for accompanying me.

Phil Parker, Atlanta, GA
1999

Dear Reader,

My journey is only one example.

Many of you have experienced changes that have shifted your lives.

I invite you to share with me those valuable lessons, insights and challenges that have had a major impact in creating **your** life's journey.

Your story may be included in a future publication. Please include your name, address and telephone number and signed permission.

Write to: going EZ enterprises
                    P.O. Box 725586
                    Atlanta, Georgia 31139

E-Mail: phil@philparker.com

RECOMMENDED READING

It's Not Over Until You Win	Les Brown
A Road Less Traveled	M. Scott Peck, M.D.
How To Get Everything You Want	Nido R. Qubein
Attitude is Everything	Paul J. Meyer
Conversations with God, 1, 2, & 3	Neale Donald Walsch
Handbook To A Happier Life	Jim Donovan
101 Ways To Promote Yourself	Raleigh Pinskey
Mutant Message Down Under	Marla Morgan
Radical Forgiveness	Colin Tipping
The Psychology of Achievement	Brian Tracey
The YES! Trilogy	Allan Somersall, Ph.D., M.D
Thinking for a Living	Joey Reiman
What Losing Taught Me About Winning	Fran Tarkenton

Ordering Information:

KISS YOURSELF *HELLO*

Single copies.........................$19.95 US / $25.95 CDN
10 or more copies................$17.95 US / $22.95 CDN

Shippng & handling:
$3.00 per single copy US
$6.00 per single copy CDN

VISA/Mastercard orders:
24-hour Voice Mail
1-800-501-8516

Or mail your order to:
going EZ enterprises
P.O. Box 725586
Atlanta, Georgia 31139

Please allow six weeks for delivery.

going EZ enterprises

Phil Parker is a professional speaker who has enlightened audiences worldwide with his creative and humorous insights. His topics include: *Life Is A Business, So Let's Get Busy; Change Is Inevitable Except From A Vending Machine* and *Lifestyle Management.* Phil has lived in Europe and traveled the world. He is a member of the National Speakers Association, the Georgia Speakers Association and Rotary International. He lives in Atlanta, Georgia with his wife Bonnie.

For information on his availability
Call Toll Free: 1-888-489-9393
Visit Phil at www.philparker.com
E-Mail: phil@philparker.com

Or Write To: Phil Parker
                    going EZ enterprises
                    P.O. Box 725586
                    Atlanta, Georgia   31139